HOW TO WRITE FOR PUBLICATION

An Introduction to Successful Freelance Writing

Graham R. Stevenson

ARROW
BUSINESS BOOKS

Arrow Books Limited 1997
10 9 8 7 6 5 4 3 2 1
© Graham R. Stevenson 1997

Arrow Books Limited
20 Vauxhall Bridge Road, London SW1V 2SA

Random House Australia (Pty) Limited
16 Dalmore Drive
Scoresby, Victoria 3179, Australia

Random House New Zealand Limited
18 Poland Road, Glenfield,
Auckland 10, New Zealand

Random House South Africa (Pty) Limited
PO Box 2263, Rosebank 2121
South Africa

Papers used by Random House UK Limited are natural,
recyclable products made from wood grown in sustainable
forests. The manufacturing processes conform to the
environmental regulations of the country of origin.

Companies, institutions and other organizations wishing
to make bulk purchases of any business books published
by Random House should contact their local bookstore
or Random House direct:
Special Sales Director
Random House
20 Vauxhall Bridge Road
London SW1V 2SA
Tel: 0171 973 9670   Fax: 0171 828 6681

Random House UK Limited Reg No. 954009

ISBN: 0 09 968511 6

Set in Sabon by
Deltatype Ltd, Birkenhead, Merseyside
Printed and bound in Great Britain by
Cox & Wyman Ltd, Reading, Berks

This book is for Maria Sozou,
who never interferes.

Contents

The idea that it is necessary to go to university
in order to become a successful writer,
or even a man or woman of letters (which is
by no means the same thing), is one of those
fantasies that surround authorship.

Vera Brittain
(1893–1970)

Introduction

Many emerging freelance writers get hooked on words without having had the benefit of some formal training. For those content to stick to the simpler areas of writing this is of little significance. Their joy at seeing a reader's letter printed in a national weekly is enough to sustain their enthusiasm.

Others come to a point where ambition takes over. Fillers no longer fulfil their need to write. They look to conquer greater challenges. Some soon discover, however, that they do not have sufficient knowledge of writing to be able to progress. The amount of study they need to correct matters is largely a question of degree. Those aiming at the Pulitzer Prize will have more to learn than those wishing to create a book about their hobby. For most, it would be wise to aim first at their hobby.

Successful writing not only depends upon literacy and a flair for words but also on the writing *process*. Fundamental questions need to be answered: How good does my English need to be? How well do I need to be presented? Where do I find an agent willing to represent me? And, if I get all this right, how much can my writing earn for me? Other questions can be more obscure. What is a preposition, for example?

The creative process consumes but a small percentage of a writer's time; perhaps less than a quarter of the overall task. Think about it for a moment. Following the basic idea for a piece, research has to be undertaken on both the subject-matter and the marketplace. When the final draft is written it will need to be presented to the target market in as attractive a package as possible. Records will need to be kept as to what has been offered and to whom. Notes of sales and of costs will need to be logged for taxation purposes. With all these functions to perform it is clear that many facets of freelance writing do not relate to creativity.

When I was editor of *Mosaic*, a small press magazine for writers, my mail often contained questions from subscribers on the writing process. In the majority, these were of a technical rather than a creative nature. It struck me that a book covering such topics would be of interest and help to emerging writers. In an endeavour to confirm this view I approached one hundred writers' circles and asked them to let me have a note of the questions most posed by their groups. I included with my enquiry a schedule of ninety-one topics designed to jog memories. These covered all aspects of writing, both creative and otherwise. Below is a representative sample of the questions posed by the groups, exactly as they were phrased:

- 'How important is good grammar?'
- 'How much can you quote from work that is still in copyright?'
- 'How does one keep to a word limit?'
- 'How long should a sentence/paragraph be?'
- 'Can a man write under a woman's name?'
- 'Does the writer decide where illustrations should go?'
- 'Is it worth buying a word processor?'
- 'What size and colour should photographs be?'
- 'Do I write to an editor first with ideas?'
- 'How long should a synopsis be?'
- 'Should one always send a cover letter, and if so, what should one say in it?'
- 'How long should you wait before you contact a publication to see if your submission will be used?'

- 'How do you choose an agent?'
- 'Does joining a writers' club really help?'

In all, over one hundred and fifty different questions were posed, covering both short and book-length topics, fiction and non-fiction, although there was a notable lack of questions associated with stage and screen. In the majority the queries raised related to topics other than the creative face of writing. By far the highest proportion covered marketing in one form or another. Others included English usage, copyright, presentation, publishing, as well as a host of other related headings.

Overall, the results of the survey showed a common need for answers to questions on the practical aspects of writing. This book sets out to fulfil that need.

An Approach To Writing

Adopting the right attitude

There is a widespread maxim in writing circles which says published writers are gifted and that their gift cannot be taught; that if you are unlucky enough to have been born without the magic ingredient you will never make it as a writer.

Such an idea is a myth.

Mastery of any business, from carpet-cleaning to bridge-building, is largely a question of approach. And writing is no exception. An organised mind coupled with a positive attitude breeds success. It is true of course, that many well-known authors *are* gifted, but saleable writing can be learned in the same way other hobbies and trades can be learned. You don't necessarily need to be gifted to become a long distance lorry driver, and in principle writing is no different. The sole qualification required to become a writer is the desire to write.

But I hear your protestations:

'My English is not up to standard. And I'll never be able to master all the intricacies of grammar.'

You don't need to. The use of 'correct' English is often flouted by well-known authors. Whilst a basic grounding in the rules is helpful, it is by no means essential. Few readers will question your grammar if your words sound right.

'I can't spell.'

Then buy a dictionary. Whenever you are unsure of a spelling, look it up. Even if that is for every other word of your writing. Constant use of a dictionary will eventually ensure accurate spelling sticks.

'I can't get ideas.'

Yes you can. Every day. Your life experience is filled with them. So is your library. Make the effort to look and ideas will follow.

'I can't compete with the professionals.'

You don't have to. There are plenty of markets open to the novice which don't attract the pros. And remember, the pros themselves were amateurs once. With practice you could step up to join them. Then you too could take on the big paying outlets.

Let's face it, the myriad of reasons many would-be writers cite as holding them back are not reasons at all. They are excuses. If you really want to write, do it. Adopt the same attitude you would in any other walk of life. If you went to see your boss for a rise, you wouldn't say: 'I don't think I'm really worth it, but I need the money.' You would use as many arguments as possible to justify your claim. Greater job experience, high inflation since your last increase. You would sell yourself. When Jeffrey Archer left politics and sat down to write his first novel *Not A Penny More, Not A Penny Less*, do you think he said to himself: 'I've never written a book before so I doubt this will be any good. But I'll write it anyway.'? Of course he didn't. He set out to produce a successful novel. When you sit down to write, you should do so with the same kind of confidence.

There are many winning attitudes towards writing. John D. MacDonald has said: 'My purpose is to entertain myself first and other people secondly.' Whilst Blaise Pascal maintained that: 'Anything that is written to please the author is worthless.' Clearly, approaches to writing vary enormously, but all can be equally successful. There is no formula to this face of writing. You simply have to have confidence in yourself.

Always think about your successes – never your failures. Positive thinking is as important in writing as it is in any other activity in life. The I'm-not-good-enough approach never won an acceptance. When you talk to your writer-friends, speak of your latest acceptance, no matter how humble an offering that may have been. Do not mention the string of rejections you may have had. Don't even think about them.

The main qualification for success is the desire for it. Those who constantly search for a magic ingredient are not being fair on themselves. There is a cliché in writing circles which says: 'Writing is one percent inspiration and ninety-nine percent perspiration.' And for the average writer that just about sums it up.

To be a writer you have to care about writing. You must want to do it. And if you want to do it badly enough, you have what it takes to become a writer. In the end, persistence will see you through. But you must be willing to learn, and to go on learning. Read everything you can on the subject of writing and associated fields. Join a writers' circle. Take a local authority evening course in creative writing. Become a member of a professional writers' organisation. Study and learn.

Having said that, there is a limit on what can be taught; essentially, you can only become a writer by writing. No amount of courses or books will overcome this hurdle for you. The more you write the better your work will become. As George Bernard Shaw once said: 'You will never write a good book until you have written some bad ones.'

A blank sheet of paper can be a daunting sight. So you need to ensure your writing environment is as conducive to productivity as possible.

A writer's life is a lonely one. Often, family do not take the aspiring writer amongst them seriously. It is important therefore to involve them as much as possible. To make them understand your needs, including the necessity for you to spend periods in isolation. Otherwise you could alienate them by your long absences. It is also possible you may one day need their help. If you reach a point where you have too many commitments to meet, they need to understand what a missed deadline means. They need to be aware of why you are unable to go late shopping *tonight*. Why you cannot cut the grass *this* weekend. Why the half-finished wallpapering needs to *stay* half-finished for a while. Why the sandwich and glass of milk will *have* to do instead of the traditional roast. Getting your family to understand such things will help you to meet deadlines. If one of them can type, or is willing to learn, so much the better. They can knock out the finished pages of a manuscript while you get on with the real writing.

It is important to find time to write regularly. Some people say they can write from nine to five. I can't do that. I need to alternate between the creative process and other tasks such as research and book-keeping. Nonetheless, I write regularly.

Ensure you arrange things so you can work uninterrupted. If you worked for an employer and one of your friends strolled into your office and asked for a cup of coffee, I suspect you would be more than a little put out. So what is different about working at home? You don't need to discipline just yourself, you need to discipline others. Ensure they don't call unannounced for a chat during your work periods. Make it known that you will be unavailable for a set period everyday.

Work in an environment that suits you. The one thing I have often heard writers say is that they either enjoy solitude or that they need to write in solitude. I enjoy both. Just being alone and writing. Indeed, I cannot write unless I am totally alone. Few people can write well when surrounded by noise and interruptions. Although there are those that find background music conducive to free expression.

Always write when it best suits you — when your mind is fresh and creative. Writers' inclinations vary a great deal. Some write 4,000 to 5,000 words per day. Others a mere 400 to 500. Some rewrite as they go. Some re-draft four or five times. Some writers are at ease composing on a keyboard, whilst others dictate into a tape recorder. Some prefer pencil and paper, others the services of a good secretary. Compose by whatever method suits you.

No matter what system you select, you will always finish with a typescript. Typewritten work can be read critically far more easily than hand-written work. You are bound to find areas needing a rewrite at this stage.

Often, beginning writers reflect upon a finished work with a sense of frustration, not knowing whether what they have written is good or bad. Books such as this can help in this respect, for they offer a degree of guidance. But the only way to know for sure whether a work is publishable is to offer it for sale. The sooner the better.

It is only by writing that you can become proficient at your craft. Keep writing and offering what you have written. Even with your speculative submissions, set yourself deadlines. And ensure you meet them. Every time you sit down to write something, make up a timetable. And stick to it. One day you may be given an editorial deadline, so break yourself into the habit now. Be ready for the real thing. Miss a commission deadline and you can forget working for that particular outlet again.

Once you have established yourself you may be lucky enough to win a regular column. If you do, you would be wise to look at other things in parallel. A publishing policy can change with a new editor or a new owner. Sometimes magazines fold. So you may suddenly find yourself without a column to write.

Success breeds success. Once you are selling regularly you can begin to think of more ambitious projects.

The step up from writing short material to full-length works can at first seem daunting. Even if you have a contract, the production of a book from the initial idea to seeing it in the shops will usually take around two years. A year to research and write, and a year to edit, publish and distribute. But don't be put off. Think of each step as an individual assignment. First the research. Then the note-taking for each chapter – each one its own contract. When you come to the writing itself, view each chapter as a separate article or short story. Such an approach can make the whole task seem so much more manageable. And remember a book takes only one basic idea. Production of the same number of words in the form of articles will take something like fifty different ideas. Viewed this way, the prospect of writing a book doesn't seem so much of a challenge.

You never know what you can achieve until you try. And writing a book can be a very rewarding experience.

Writer's block

Most writers suffer from a loss of output from time to time. Often without apparent reason. But there are methods and some tricks available to overcome this state of inactivity.

Writer's block can take two forms:

- The inability to think up an initial idea
- A sticking point in the middle of a piece which has seen a successful start

So what can be done to stimulate initial ideas?

The first thing to do is to examine what you know. Your hobby, your job, your home town, your friends, your pets, your everyday experiences. What you have read, the films you have seen, what you have overheard on the bus, the places you have visited, the people you have met. All of these are raw materials for your writing. Be aware. Be continually on the lookout for ideas. What do you talk about with your friends? What is the topic of chat in the office? If it is of sufficient interest for your colleagues to talk about it, it may just make the theme for a saleable article or short story.

Another approach is to concentrate on a single idea or phrase, and to develop it. Take birthdays, for example. Target any month in the year and research the birthdays of some famous people. The slant to such a piece could be the vast differences between personalities born at the same time of year. Is there truth in astrology?

Let's examine another such idea. This time, let us look at news. It is often said that truth is stranger than fiction. Can this be so? Examine a few national and regional newspapers and magazines and you will soon discover that it can. Have a look at this story appearing in *Family Tree Magazine*:

> In the course of a drive to repossess overdue library books, Miss Sandra Wilkinson of Durham called at the house of a borrower who admitted she had failed to return three rebound paperbacks. This was, she said, because the undertaker who called at her house when her husband died had used them to prop up the deceased's head in his coffin and they had been buried with him.

There has to be a short story plot here somewhere!

Now, think about some of the following to see how they could be developed:

- Anniversaries
- Clichés
- Eponyms (people whose names are given to places, tribes or institutions)
- Euphemisms (substitution of mild or pleasant terms for those that are offensive or blunt)
- Fallacies
- Inventions
- Mottoes
- Slang
- Sun signs
- Superstitions
- Topicality
- Toponyms (place-names)

If you still have trouble finding ideas, simply begin writing. Anything.

Take a blank sheet of paper and a pen, and sit down to write. Write the first thing that enters your head. Just one word will do for a start. Ask yourself questions about that word. Suppose your word happened to be: *clock*. Is it a new clock or an old clock? Let us select an old clock. A grandfather clock? Ornate and finely inlaid perhaps. They can be rare enough to be collectors' items. Antiques of this nature can fetch tens of thousands of pounds. Where can they be bought and sold? Where can they be repaired and restored? Is it a difficult trade to learn? A piece about grandfather clocks could be slanted to suit many non-fiction markets:

- Antique collectors' magazines
- Investment magazines
- Hobby magazines
- Country magazines

A grandfather clock could also feature in fiction. It could be the focal point in a romance, for example. The stained glass door to the pendulum compartment could be the dropping-off point for secret love letters, perhaps.

Or it could be the basis of a thriller. A secret compartment could be made to contain drugs or counterfeit bonds.

No matter which method you use to conjure ideas, always write them down. Keep a book of all your thoughts. Ideas are valuable, so don't allow forgetfulness to lose you any.

Before you begin to write up any of your ideas ensure you have given them plenty of thought. In my early days as a writer, ideas were so hard to come by that when they did surface they were precious to me. So much so that when an idea came into my mind I would sit down to write and try to get the whole piece written as quickly as I could. At that time I held the view that inspiration strikes so seldom that it should be exploited before it has the chance to fade and disappear. I still ensure I don't forget ideas by making a note of them, but now that I have gained experience I never begin a piece straight away. I carry the idea around in my head for a while to see what develops. Sometimes, the piece goes in a totally different direction to my original thinking. Usually for the better. At other times, my initial thoughts multiply so that one idea can be slanted in more than one direction to create material for two or more pieces. I suggest you treat ideas in the same way. Mull them over to see if you can slant them into several pieces.

Sometimes, as I write articles and stories, they flow onto paper at the first attempt. At other times, I have to work at it. I write a bit here, a bit there. Fill something in the middle. Shuffle things around. Come to a full-stop and have to abandon work. Come back to it later and still have writer's block. Eventually, I get to the point I want to be. I then rewrite and rewrite again. And then again if I have to. In the end, these reworked pieces turn out fine. As good, sometimes better, than those which flow straight off the pen at the first sitting. But no matter how well thought out a piece may be, writer's block can strike at any time without apparent reason.

You are far less likely to encounter writer's block if you work to a synopsis. Beginning from cold is asking for trouble. Start your writing with a plan. Beginning, middle and end. First, make a list of all the points you wish to include. Then arrange them into a coherent order. The simple act of putting things into sequence can get your writing motor going. In itself, it is an excellent way of overcoming writer's block.

Write the way you talk. A conversational style flows easily from one point to another. You think in pictures, and if you write this way, your words will be clear. Writers often come to a full-stop when composing on paper, but it is doubtful they would reach this point in mid-conversation.

Another way to get ideas and overcome writer's block is to seek the help of a collaborator.

Collaboration

Some writers feel they produce their best work when working

with someone else. A joint venture is the catalyst they need to produce saleable work. This approach will not suit everyone, of course, for as Evelyn Waugh once said: 'I never can understand how two men can write a book together; to me that's like three people getting together to have a baby.' If you hold this view you will need to stick to solo work. For others, collaboration can provide the stimulus they need. Comedy writer Barry Cryer, for example, often works with a co-writer because ideas come easier to him that way. If you believe you could produce more and better work this way you should give it a try. But first you will need to examine your basic motivation for writing. Are you writing for the love of writing, or are you looking to make a profit from the venture? If you write simply for the love of it, you can collaborate at any level, provided you can find a willing partner. Articles, short stories, even fillers can be written to good effect as a joint venture. But don't expect to get rich this way. By the time you have deducted joint expenses from your earnings you will be lucky to break even. Those seeking to produce book-length works could make collaboration pay.

Collaboration can work wonders for your output. You can produce a great deal you would never have written alone. You might be a writer or you might be an ideas person. Either way, the thoughts of one partner can spark off ideas in the other; ideas that you wouldn't otherwise have had.

The skills you need to look for in a collaborator will depend upon your own ability. You may be a good researcher but a poor writer. You may have an idea for a non-fiction book but not the necessary skill to be able to produce the text for it. So you go in search of someone who has. Alternatively, you may decide to collaborate with an expert in the field who can give you the facts and figures whilst you do the writing. If you wish to produce a biography, the subject of the book could be your collaborator by supplying you with the facts about his life. Sometimes too, a writer, having no draughting skills of his own, will need to collaborate with an illustrator.

Once you have decided what skills you are looking for in a partner, you will need to seek him/her out. If you are looking for a writer to produce work as a hobby you could try contacting your nearest amateur writers' group. If you have difficulty locating one, take a look at the *Directory of Writers' Circles* published by Laurence Pollinger Ltd. Alternatively, the amateur could try advertising in one of the small press magazines devoted to freelance writing such as *Quartos* or *Writer's Own*.

The more serious scribe, looking to produce a book-length work on a commercial basis, could advertise for a partner in one of the up-market writers' magazines. Perhaps the most well known of these is *The Author*, the journal of The Society of Authors. Or you could try one of the other writing magazines, such as *Freelance Writing and Photography*, *Writer's Monthly* or *Writers News*.

Your *Yellow Pages* could also be the source of what you are looking for. See under 'Journalists', 'Newspaper Correspondents' and 'Writers'.

Another way to locate a professional writer is to examine magazines and newsletters devoted to the subject of your proposed book. Note the names of the contributors and write to them care of the publication in which they appear. They may just be in the market for some extra work. This approach can also be used by the writer looking for a collaborator to supply the raw material. It is likely that authors appearing in specialist magazines will have the specialist knowledge you seek. Again, you could write to them care of the magazine, or alternatively you could place an advertisement in the classified columns.

Specialist knowledge can also be sought via clubs, circles, and organisations dealing with the subject you wish to cover. A short note to the membership secretary asking how you can contact members willing to impart their knowledge to you is likely to bring a good response. People like to talk about their specialist subject. They will be flattered you consider them to be an expert in the field.

Once you have your offer of help, choose your partner with care. Not only will you need to ensure they have the knowledge you seek, but also that they have the right attitude. As Agatha Christie once said: 'I've always believed in writing without a collaborator, because where two people are writing the same book, each believes he gets all the worries and only half the royalties.'

Try to ensure your chosen partner is sympathetic to your needs and is someone you would be happy to work with. Ask yourself some pertinent questions: Does he/she possess the right knowledge? Is it up to date? Will he/she be dependable? Does he/she smoke or drink? Can you understand his/her accent? Will he/she allow you sufficient freedom of expression? Are you going to work at his/her place, or yours? Does he/she live near enough for you to meet with ease?

When you come to meet your prospective candidate, check evidence of qualifications or samples of published work and examine his/her approach to your meeting. A casual attitude towards your meeting may mean he/she is casual about writing.

Remember too, it is a mutual exercise. He/she will be weighing you up as well, so it is important that you portray professionalism. Sell yourself. But be honest about what you can and cannot do. Show some samples of your work. When your meeting is at an end, don't make a decision there and then, say you will be in touch shortly.

Even when you have chosen your co-worker, difficulties can still creep in. Collaboration has its risks. You may choose a partner who isn't up to the job, no matter how impressive he/she may have been at the interview. On the other hand, he/she may be knowledgeable enough, but you have disagreements on what should be left in and what should be left out. For example, the merits, or otherwise of choosing illustrations, the direction of style and readability. You will need to be diplomatic over such matters. Once you have an agreement with a collaborator you are stuck with him/her for the duration of the project. So make the most of it.

Ensure you have a written agreement drawn up before you begin your writing task. Include who will be responsible for what. And how the proceeds will be divided up between you. But before you decide, examine how much effort your partner is going to expend in comparison with your own. If you are collaborating with an expert, he/she may have all the knowledge which is to form the basis of the book, but remember how much work *you* will have to do. You will be responsible for the actual writing, the typing and the editing. Determine what would be a fair split. Is it a 50/50 arrangement, a 20/80 arrangement, or would 80/20 be fairer?

Your collaborator may have no knowledge of the writing process, so that you, the writer, do most of the work. Under these circumstances it would only be fair that you got the larger percentage of the take – say 60/40. It could be though, that whilst an expert has a small input to your book, you would have no book without it. You need his/her expert knowledge to be able to proceed. In these circumstances, he/she may be able to demand a disproportionately high percentage of the royalties. And if you want to write the book you will have to go along with such a deal.

If you wish to work with a photographer or artist, his/her percentage input would influence his/her share of the proceeds. If illustrations form a large part of the book, it may be that he/she should get a bigger cut than you. On the other hand, if there are only two or three illustrations he/she may get as low as a 10% cut. (In these circumstances you should ask yourself whether a collaboration arrangement is the right approach – perhaps a flat fee would be better.)

Once you have made up your mind what is fair, ensure your collaborator agrees with your assessment and have it included in the agreement. Ensure your programme for the book is mutually agreed and that it fits in with all holiday, business, and other commitments. Once you have all the details sorted out, see a solicitor and have a formal agreement drawn up.

The mechanics of writing

The creative process is the most important of the writer's activities, so it should be allotted the most suitable time in your schedule; when your mind is at its freshest. This period will not be the same for all people, of course. Some minds work at their best first thing in the morning, whilst others rise to the occasion late at night. You should stick to the time that suits you. You are the kind of person you are; if you are a night owl, don't try to be a lark.

Concentration levels vary from one individual to another. For myself, I cannot undertake the creative side of writing for more than two to three hours at a stretch. I then break off to attend to some other facet of the business, such as typing, filing or perhaps some research. I am not alone in this respect, for many writers find the creative process a drain. Anthony Trollope once said: 'Three hours a day will produce as much as a man ought to write.' Not all are of this disposition, of course. Arthur Hailey has said he commences writing at 6 a.m. and goes through to 4.30 or 5 p.m., stopping only for breakfast and lunch. I believe people of such ability to be rare. It is important therefore, for us mere mortals to organise our other writing activities to fit available periods in order to make the best possible use of our time.

Established writers will have several pieces on the go at once. They'll probably all be at a different stage of development at any one time. This holds the advantage that you can spread time between them. It is therefore wise to set aside specific periods each day for different authoring tasks. When your creative motor has expired, switch to something less demanding. Allow time for each of these activities:

- Market research
- Subject research
- Organising notes
- Writing a first draft
- Typing the first draft

- Rewriting
- Researching and producing illustrations
- Retyping
- Correspondence
- Book-keeping

If you alternate these activities on a daily basis, you will keep your mind fresh, ensuring you use your time to its fullest advantage.

Keeping time

Many part-time freelance writers write on spec. They complete a piece then offer it for publication. Even the more experienced writer concentrating on short stories will work this way. But the more professional freelance, concentrating on short non-fiction, will try to sell a piece before it is written. He/she will sell the *idea* behind it first. If he/she can interest an editor, he/she may receive a commission to write the piece. He/she will then produce it to the editor's preferred length and will incorporate any comments or guidelines that have been offered.

Often, a commissioning editor will give a deadline for the submission. If it is a tight one, you may have to adopt a flexible approach to your other writing activities. In the extreme, you may have to concentrate on nothing but that one piece until it is finished.

No matter how generous the lead, you will need to plan your production in order to monitor whether or not you are keeping to time. Let us look at a 2,000 word article.

How long it will take you to write it will depend upon several factors, not the least of which will be the rate at which you can compose. As we said earlier, outputs vary enormously from one person to another. Upton Sinclair is said to have composed 8,000 words per day. Charlotte Lamb has been attributed with the ability to write as many as 15,000 words per day at her peak. I find such figures difficult to believe, but even at half this quoted output, theirs is fast writing indeed. At the other end of the scale we have a personality such as Arthur Hailey, who produces only 600 to 1,000 words per day, despite the long hours he works. Be realistic about your own ability; if 500 words per day is the best you can do, target at 400. Give yourself breathing space.

Now consider the other tasks necessary to meet your deadline. There will be no need for market research; you will have done that before you sent your query. You will also have done some, if not all, of your subject research. Allow a day for this in case you have to delve for a fact you have overlooked.

How long will it take to put your facts into their proper sequence? To a large degree, this will depend upon how well you know your subject. If it is one close to your heart, much of the theme of the piece will be in your head and so will fall into sequence with little effort. A well researched subject outside of your own knowledge will consist of many notes. These will take time to put into order. Let's allow a day.

When you have your first draft written, you will need to type it. Many amateur writers are self-taught typists, and not the best. Let us allow 20 words per minute plus 100% for alterations. A total of say, half a day. You'll need the same for the final manuscript after revision.

Once you have your first draft typewritten, you will need to edit it and to put the polish onto it. How long this will take will depend on how much rewriting you usually need to do. Some writers rewrite a great deal at the longhand stage. Others, during the first draft revision. Only you can make the estimate. For our purpose, let us allow one day.

To determine what all this means, let us look at it pictorially. See *Fig. 1*.

Overall, you will need nine days to produce the article at your normal rate of output. Now comes the loaded question: what if your target editor asks you to do it quicker? Then you have to ask

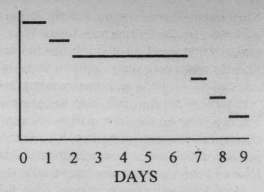

Subject Research
Assemble Facts
Write First Draft
Type First Draft
Rewrite
Retype

0 1 2 3 4 5 6 7 8 9

DAYS

Fig 1. A typical schedule for writing an article.

yourself whether you are prepared to burn the midnight oil. If you are, and you still decide to go ahead, at least you'll have a good idea of what is ahead of you.

Word counts

If a writer is to see his/her work published, he/she must first get to grips with accurate word counts. There are four main reasons for word counts:

- To assess the length of articles and short stories in market research.
- To write articles and short stories to a pre-determined length limit.
- To assess the length of books in market research.
- To write books to a pre-determined length limit.

To assess the length of an article or a short story, count the first one hundred words and mark the page. This will establish how much space the one hundred words occupies. Make a measure of this space on a strip of paper and use it to mark off the full length of your chosen piece at one hundred word intervals, making allowance for headings, sub-headings and illustrations as you go. To estimate the total length of the piece, count the number of spaces marked off and multiply by one hundred. This will provide a reasonably accurate guide to the length of the piece, particularly if you bear in mind that preferred editorial lengths are usually to a round hundred, e.g. 500, 800, 1,000 etc. Carry out this exercise on several pieces in successive issues of a title to ensure they are generally the same length. Finally, when you have assessed three or four articles for the same market, count every word of one of them to confirm your assessment.

Many beginners have difficulty writing to a specified length limit, but if you are to see your work published this is a hurdle you must overcome. Editors plan to strict space restrictions and you will have to comply with their requirements if you want your work to sell. It would be pointless to submit a work of 800 words to a market using only pieces of 1,000 words. No matter how good your writing such a submission would not be published.

It is a good idea to make a word count as you write. I write in longhand (despite owning a word processor I still prefer this method for the first draft) and upon completion of each page I go over what I have written and count every word. I then write the number of words at the foot of the page. This way I can keep a running total as I go. As my handwriting is very small, an A4 page averages out at 500 words. A 2,000 word piece therefore occupies about four full pages. This fact is a good check on my word count.

When you get to typing the first draft, assessment becomes a little easier. A typical page arranged double spaced in manuscript form will contain, on average, 230 words.

Once you have rewritten the draft manuscript, you will need to accurately check it for length. If your typescript has been produced on a typewriter this will involve counting every word. Those fortunate enough to possess a word processor may have the facility in the computer software to count the words (more about this later). At this stage you will need to ensure your total count is within 5% of your target ideal. Anything outside of this will not find editorial favour. Show your word count to the nearest 50 words on the front sheet of your manuscript.

Market research to determine length is just as important for books as it is for shorter works. How long a book should be will depend upon several factors, not the least of which will be your market. This is particularly so for genre works, both fiction and non-fiction. Romantic novels frequently fall into this category, as do non-fiction books forming a series. For these you must stick to a strict word limit.

One-off books won't need such a rigid approach. Within limits, these can be as long as they need to be. In practice, it is difficult to make a work of less than 35,000 words look like a book (unless there are numerous illustrations to take up space). So, this is often thought of as the minimum length a book should be. Works of 25,000 words do make it into print, but they are the rare exception.

Upper limits for non-genre books seem to be stretching, particularly for the well-known author of fiction. Not so long ago, 60,000 was typical. Today, works of 200,000 words are commonplace.

Children's books vary from just a few words to several thousand depending upon the age group. A study of previously published works covering your target audience is therefore essential.

Books usually contain a specific number of pages because, often, they are made up of multiples of large folded sheets which themselves make 16 pages. Books are therefore made up of 16 page increments. For example: 96, 112, 128, 144, etc. With modern techniques this is not always the case, but it still holds good for many processes. For this reason, it is important with book-length works to indicate to the publisher how many pages your manuscript will occupy. Whilst a word count is important, it will need to be looked at in conjunction with the number of headings, sub-headings and illustrations.

Once you have decided how long your book is to be, you will need to write it to that length and stick to it. The first thing to do is to break it down into manageable elements. Let us look at a target of 50,000 words in 10 chapters. That is 5,000 words per chapter. Let us say there are to be an average of 5 sub-headings per chapter. That is an average of 1,000 words for each of 50 sub-headings. If you count each page of your draft, you can keep track of how close you are to your target. When one section is too long or too short, you can adjust future sections to compensate.

2

Getting The Words Right

Tools of the trade

The most common way to communicate is by the use of words. Words are the raw material of language. They may be either written or spoken. Our concern is with written words, for they are the tools of the writing profession.

Words are powerful. The greater our command of them, the more compelling our writing is likely to be. As Rudyard Kipling once said: 'Words are the most powerful drug used by mankind.' Other writers feel likewise. Edward Thorndike once said: 'Colours fade, temples crumble, empires fall, but wise words endure.' And Eddie Canter maintained that: '. . . browsing in a dictionary is like being turned loose in a bank.'

It is clear that a writer's vocabulary cannot be too large. This isn't to say saleable writing cannot be achieved with just a limited vocabulary. Writing simply becomes easier as a broader knowledge of words is acquired.

Obtain some reference works. A good dictionary and a thesaurus are essential tools of the trade. Those specialising in verse will also need a rhyming dictionary. And the puzzle compiler cannot do without a crossword dictionary.

Get used to learning new words. Particularly by reading. Whenever you come across a word new to you, look it up in your dictionary. Similarly, when writing, if a word appropriate to express your thoughts does not spring to mind, reach for your thesaurus. Get to know the precise meaning of words, particularly those that sound alike. If you write technical pieces, ensure you use the correct jargon. Technical terms change with the times, and new raw materials and manufacturing processes are being discovered almost every day. Keep up to date.

Once you have begun to broaden your vocabulary, be wary of how you use it. Whilst it is a helpful tool, a large vocabulary should not mean you necessarily use long words – far from it. As Mark Twain once said: 'I never written *metropolis* for seven cents because I can get the same price for *city*. I never write *policeman* because I can get the same money for *cop*.' He had a point. And doubtless he had his target readership in mind when he made such a statement.

Writing cluttered with obscure words won't be read. Whilst you, the writer, will reach for your dictionary when you come across a word you don't understand, the average reader will not. They will simply become irritated. If they come across a second which is not understood they are likely to stop reading. Never try to impress with clever words. A large vocabulary alone will not make you into a published writer. Nor will a command of grammar. Writing may be grammatically correct, the spelling perfect, but if it does not entertain who will read it?

Writers who try to be 'literary' can sound stilted and unnatural. Beginners often worry too much about the correct use of grammar. Until, that is, they learn that a great deal of popular published writing is riddled with grammatical errors. Too many beginners believe they need to be literary when they simply need to be themselves; to let their personality shine through.

Often apprentice writers cling to what they were taught during their formative years: sets of unbreakable rules. It is wise to abandon this approach if you are to give your writing readability and style. For example, it is said a sentence should not end with a preposition. But this 'rule' can be limiting. As Winston Churchill once said when a sentence of his had been criticised because it broke this law: 'This is the sort of English up with which I will not put.' I think he made the point rather nicely. For the sake of readability it is sometimes better to break the 'rules'.

Many people have never had the benefit of formal training in grammar, or if they had, they have long since forgotten it. But their use of English is often better than they imagine. Automatically, they know not to say: 'They wasn't there.' They may not know the reason why such a statement is incorrect. They have learnt grammar by example – by reading magazines, newspapers and books, and from their everyday conversations. Nevertheless, these people are inhibited about their writing because they feel they lack a knowledge of the rules.

It is natural for the emerging writer to have some interest in grammar, even if that interest is simply to know whether or not you are following the rules. But you would be wise not to be *overly* concerned about it. If your writing is easy to read and your reader does not constantly have to stop to think about its meaning, then you are a successful writer. Even the greats of literature break the rules, and clearly they are content that they do. Raymond Chandler once said in a letter to his English publisher: 'When I split an infinitive, god damn it, I split it so that it stays split!' And Jay Dean, the US baseball player turned writer, once said when criticised about his misuse of grammar: 'A lot of people who don't say *ain't* ain't eatin'.'

The test of good writing is its readability and whether or not it communicates what you want to say. 'Good' writing is a question of degree. Most aspiring scribes want to get on with the business of writing – to get words onto paper. Trying to think of correct grammar as you write can inhibit flow. That doesn't mean you should be sloppy – if you are keen enough you will seek to improve your knowledge of your craft at all times.

Below is an outline of the rules. It is not definitive, just an outline. Hopefully, it will encourage the newcomer not to be intimidated by it in future writings.

English grammar

English has seen many stages of development from Anglo-Saxon times, being influenced from outside forces such as our domination by the Romans and later the Vikings and Normans. Different dialects emerged, and even today they still exist. The dialect of London eventually emerged as Standard English.

In Standard English all words fall into categories called *parts of speech*. These are the noun, pronoun, adjective, verb, adverb, preposition, conjunction, interjection.

Noun

A noun is a word used as the name of a person, place, thing or quality. For example: *girl, man, Jane, London, Australia, Brighton, garden, house, anger*. There are four kinds of noun:

Proper nouns: These name *particular* people, places, or things. These include the names of people, towns, countries, streets, companies, months of the year. Proper nouns always begin with a capital letter. The following are proper nouns: *Frank Sinatra, Winchester Cathedral, Oxford Street, Wednesday, Easter, Woolworths*.

Collective nouns: These are names of groups of things. For example: *flock, crowd, team, gang, fleet*.

Abstract nouns: These are names of qualities; intangibles. For example: *light, curiosity, energy, choice, health, peace*.

Common nouns: These are names shared in common by all things of the same kind. For example: *bus, bottle, book, dog, town, woman*.

Pronoun

Pronouns are words used instead of nouns. They identify people and things without specifically naming them. For example: *I, we, they, it, he, she, him, them, us.* Pronouns do the same job as nouns.

Examine this sentence:

The ball bounced across the road and *it* hit a car.

Here, *it* is the pronoun used instead of the noun *ball*.

Examine another example:

Paul and Rose went to the party where *they* danced a lot.

Here, the pronoun *they* replaces the nouns *Paul* and *Rose*.

Adjective

An adjective is a word naming a quality, added to a noun to describe the thing more fully. For example:

The *massive* guns fired out to sea.
The *green* door stood ajar.
A *slim* girl entered the room.
The plate was *warm*.

The italicised words are the adjective naming a quality of the nouns *guns, door, girl, plate.*

Adjectives tell us more about nouns in different ways. The most common adjectives **describe** the noun: *red* carpet, *steep* hill, *bright* star, *popular* singer.

Adjectives can also indicate **quantity**: *twenty* cars, *several* people, *few* successes, *nine* actors.

Some adjectives indicate **possession**: *his* hat, *my* bicycle, *its* hair, *their* house.

Other adjectives **demonstrate** the noun: *that* book, *those* people, *this* place, *these* cups.

Adjectives can also be **interrogative:** *Which* house do you live in? *What* did you say? *Whose* book is this? *Why* are you leaving?

Verb
A verb is a word that expresses action or being. It makes a statement about the subject of a sentence. For example:

My father *walked* to church.
The dog *swam* to the ball.
My neighbour *is* American.
The cups *are* full.

In the first two sentences, the verbs express action. In the other two sentences the verbs express being.

A verb may consist of more than one word, as in these two examples: He *was walking* to school. They *were offered* tea.

Adverb
An adverb adds to the meaning of a verb:

The man walked *unsteadily*.

Here, *unsteadily* is the adverb which adds to the meaning of the verb *walked*.

Paul drove *quickly*.

Here, *quickly* is the adverb which adds to the meaning of the verb *drove*.

Helen arrived *early*.

Here, *early* is the adverb which adds to the meaning of the verb *arrived*.

He closed the door *noisily*.

Here, *noisily* is the adverb which adds to the meaning of the word *closed*.

An adjective can also add to the meaning of other adjectives and other adverbs.

This is a *very* hot day.

Here, *very* is the adverb describing the adjective *hot*.

He dances *exceptionally* well.

Here, the adverb *well* adds to the meaning of the verb *dances*. *Exceptionally* also acts as an adverb as it adds to the meaning of *well*.

Preposition
A preposition is a word governing a noun or pronoun to indicate the relationship of one word with another. These are prepositions: *of, after, until, below, amongst*.

Look at these examples:

They live *in* a bungalow.
The tiles *on* the roof are loose.
I found Paul *at* home.
The ball came *through* the window.

Conjunction
A conjunction is a word used to connect words or phrases. These are conjunctions: *and, but, or, if, because*.

Look at these examples:

The beer was weak *and* it was warm.
They travelled by road *and* by rail.
The food was cold *but* tasty.
The house was *neither* clean *nor* tidy.

Interjection

An interjection is an exclamatory word or phrase *interjected* to express feeling. Interjections play no part in the grammar of a sentence. These are interjections: *Ah! Indeed! Gosh! OK!*

Look at these examples:

'*Ah!* so you found it.'
'I did, *indeed!*'
'*What a shame*, he didn't make it.'
'*Why!* he failed again.'

Note: Some words have different meanings and can change their grammatical function from one sentence to another. For example, *sink* can be either a noun or a verb, as in these two sentences:

Dirty crockery filled the *sink*. (noun)
The frogman swam out to *sink* the ship. (verb)

Sentences

Written communication is made up of *sentences*. A sentence is a group of words which make sense. Consider the following:

in the garden
underneath the tree
on the table
the red car

These groups of words do not make sentences because they do not make complete sense; they do not express a complete idea. They are *phrases*. Whilst not making complete sense on their own, each of these groups of words can be used as part of larger word groups that do make sense. Consider these:

Paul was *in the garden*.
The deckchair stood *underneath the tree*.
The teapot was *on the table*.
The red car stopped at the traffic lights.

Each of these groups of words now makes complete sense. Word groups that make complete sense are known as *sentences*. A sentence can stand alone and needs nothing added to it to complete its meaning.

Every sentence consists of two parts: a *subject*, and a *predicate*. The subject is a word, or group of words, that names the person or thing the sentence is about. The rest of the sentence, the predicate, says something about the subject. Consider this sentence:

She wore a red dress.

Here, *She* is the subject, the remainder of the sentence is the predicate.

As we have said, a sentence is a group of words which makes complete sense. To do this it must contain, at least, a subject and a verb. A *phrase* does not contain a verb. Consider this sentence:

He went to the races.

Here, *He* is the subject and *went* is the verb.

Whilst sentences make sense in themselves, not all sentences have the same function. There are four forms of sentence: a statement, a command, a question and an exclamation. For example:

The car is standing outside the station.
Go to school.
Where is the newspaper?
I hate this rain!

A sentence may be either simple or compound. A simple sentence makes one statement and has one verb. For example:

The boat was in the water.

This sentence makes one statement and has one verb, *was*. It is a simple sentence.

Now consider these two sentences:

The car stopped.
The traffic lights were red.

Each of these is a sentence in its own right. Each has a subject and a predicate. They can be joined together and still form a sentence:

The car stopped because the traffic lights were red.

This sentence now has two subjects and two predicates. It is a *compound* sentence. The two original sentences have become *clauses*. When a simple sentence becomes part of a longer sentence it becomes a *clause*. A compound sentence is composed of two or more clauses connected together.

A useful device for joining sentences is the relative pronoun, such as *who, whom, whose, which, that*. For example:

He was a wicked man. He would steal from his own mother.
He was a wicked man *who* would steal from his own mother.

By now, you may be wondering about one word sentences. They crop up everywhere: *'Yes.' 'Maybe.' 'What?' 'Steady!' 'Wait!'* If the simplest of sentences has a subject and a predicate, how can one word make a sentence? Well, technically it cannot. In practice, the missing part of the sentence is *implied*. For example:

'What?' really means: *'What did you say?'*

'*Wait!*' really means: '*You wait!*'

As we have seen, sentences may be long or short. But complicated sentences should be avoided. A sentence should contain a single thought or idea. This way your reader will have no difficulty understanding it. If a sentence isn't clear, rewrite it until it is.

Paragraphs

A piece of writing is made up of a number of thoughts and ideas and these need to be arranged in a logical sequence. Each paragraph is a progression in that sequence.

The beginning of a new paragraph indicates a change in ideas, or a change in slant to an idea. Each paragraph should deal with one aspect of the subject. When moving from one aspect to another, the two should be dealt with separately in separate paragraphs.

A paragraph consists of a major unit of information. It may consist of one sentence or several sentences. Having said that, paragraph lengths are also about markets. It is pointless to write a long paragraph when your target market uses only short ones. Tabloid newspapers, for example, are often composed entirely of very short paragraphs.

It is better to have too many paragraphs than too few. Short paragraphs help to break up the monotony of reading. Many readers are intimidated by long paragraphs.

A very long paragraph can be broken down into two or more shorter paragraphs provided there is a link to associate them to the theme of the original paragraph.

The one time you should *always* begin a new paragraph is when there is a change of speaker in dialogue.

Punctuation

Punctuation marks are available as an aid to reading. They do not follow a set of unbreakable rules. Their prime function is to make writing clear and unambiguous.

In speech, we use pauses and inflexions to make ourselves clearly understood. The pauses vary in length and the inflexions change in tone with different intended meanings. In order to convey these to the written word we use punctuation. As a rough guide, a comma signals a pause of one, a semi-colon a pause of two, a colon a pause of three, a full stop a pause of four. The pause for an exclamation mark or a question mark is roughly the same as the full stop. It is natural for the voice to fall in tone at the end of a sentence, unless the sentence is a question or an exclamation. The voice tends to rise in pitch when asking a question, and is more forceful when uttering an exclamation.

Punctuation gives writing rhythm. It also helps to avoid ambiguity. Take this passage from the *Westmorland Gazette*:

Magnificent country residence approached by a private drive with full gas central heating.

Is the drive really centrally heated, I wonder? If the composer of this passage had included a parenthesis, his intended meaning would have been conveyed without ambiguity:

Magnificent country residence (approached by a private drive) with full gas central heating.

The BBC's Ceefax news service could also have taken a lesson in punctuation when they broadcast this:

Veteran Northampton second row forward Vince Cannon has retired one season early after 438 games with a back injury.

Mr. Cannon certainly is a glutton for punishment – 438 games with a back injury! Add two commas and the true meaning is apparent:

Veteran Northampton second row forward Vince Cannon has retired one season early, after 438 games, with a back injury.

One advertiser in the *Evesham Admag* could use a lesson or two:

Man's bicycle, needs minor repairs, plus parts of ladies.

I wonder which parts of the ladies are up for grabs: arms or legs. And I thought Jack the Ripper had left this earth long ago. Try this:

Man's bicycle, needs minor repairs, plus parts of lady's.

Sensible punctuation creates unambiguous writing. A simple test is to read your words aloud and note the pauses. Then punctuate your writing to suit.

The Full Stop
We saw earlier, that there are four forms of sentence: a statement, a question, a command, an exclamation. A full stop is used to indicate the end of a sentence which is neither a question nor an exclamation.

A full stop is also used after an abbreviation. For example: Mr., Mrs., Dr., U.K., B.B.C., N.A.T.O.

When an abbreviation ends a sentence, one full stop is enough to indicate both the abbreviation and the end of the sentence. For example:

Martin Smith was a resident of the U.K.

It is becoming increasingly popular however, to omit full stops in abbreviations, like so: Mr, Mrs, Dr, UK, BBC, NATO.

The Comma
Some writers have a tendency to overuse commas. The test, as we

said earlier, is to ask yourself if your intended meaning would be clear without them. Their inclusion, or omission, can completely change the meaning of a sentence:

> The visitor said Jim came from London.
> The visitor, said Jim, came from London.

Commas can be used to separate a comment that interrupts the continuity of a sentence:

> Paul, losing control, shouted at Keith.
> Sheila took the cup of coffee, which was now cold, over to the sink.

Commas can also take the place of brackets:

> The apparatus (which we described earlier) is now ready for use.
> The apparatus, which we described earlier, is now ready for use.

Commas can be used to separate items on a list:

> Many sporting events are sponsored by public companies. Among these are: horse racing, snooker, tennis, motor cross, and speedway.

Whether or not there should be a comma before the 'and' is a question of preference. Some publishing houses like it, others do not.

In speech, a comma is used before and after the name of a person:

> 'Paul, where have you been?'
> 'Hello, chum, have you been here long?'

A comma is also used before and after speech which is attributed to a person:

'Please don't go,' she pleaded.

Note: A capital letter is needed at the beginning of speech, even if it has been preceded by another part of the sentence:

He said, 'That is mine.'

Also note that no capital letter is needed when the speech continues after an interruption:

'Before you go,' he begged, 'have another drink.'

The Semicolon

Sometimes, two sentences are closely related in meaning. On these occasions a semicolon can be used instead of a full stop. What precedes and what follows a semicolon should be a grammatically complete sentence (or *inferred* to be a complete sentence). In other words, a semicolon can be used to link *clauses* that are closely related in meaning. For example:

When in Rome, do as the Romans do; when in England, do as you please.

In joining closely related clauses, the semicolon can also take the place of link words such as *and, but, which*. For example:

The defendant was given a three month prison sentence; suspended for two years.

The Colon

A colon indicates a close connection between the words it separates, particularly when it is used to amplify a statement. For example:

He gave her what she had longed for: a gold ring.

A colon is often used to introduce a series of items:

The committee was made up of members of many nations: Brazil, Canada, U.S.A., Greenland, Algeria, Zaire.

A colon can also be used to introduce a quotation:

Brian held up his hand and said: 'Wait right there!'

It should be noted however, that it is more usual to use a comma in this context:

Brian held up his hand and said, 'Wait right there!'

A colon is also used before an explanation:

There were three main reasons for his change of job: a better salary, a better company car, a shorter journey from home.

The Question Mark
A question mark is used to indicate a direct question:

'Where is the bus stop?'
'Can I have another cake, please?'

A question mark can also be used to transform a group of words used in dialogue from a statement into a question:

'It really wasn't meant to happen?'
'He didn't stop at the red light?'

No question mark is used in indirect speech:

He asked for a drink.
The question of where the dog had gone nagged him.

The Exclamation Mark
The exclamation mark is used after exclamations, such as:

'Gosh!'
'Good heavens!'
'I don't believe it!'
'No chance!'

An exclamation mark is also used to denote shock or surprise:

'He had the cheek to say I wasn't up to the job!'
'It turned out to be as big as a bus!'

Whilst the use of exclamation marks is sometimes necessary, they should be used sparingly. Over-use of them has the reverse of the desired effect so that writing loses its impact. Over-use can also be tiresome – even irritating. Used sparingly they can be very effective.

The Hyphen
A hyphen can be used to link separate words to make a compound which has a special meaning when formed: walking-stick, key-ring, feather-bed, stunt-man.

In the first of these examples, the hyphen not only shows a close link between the two words, it also avoids the absurd statement that would be made without it – since when has a stick been able to walk?

A hyphen is often used to separate parts of a word. This is done when it would be difficult to immediately understand a word without it. This is often the case with words beginning with *co*: co-operate, co-ordinate, co-axial, co-educational.

A hyphen is also used when a word has to be broken at the end of a line because there is insufficient room to complete it. It is the convention in such cases, to break the word where there is a natural pause in speech. If *partition* needed to be broken, the best place to break it would be after the *r*: par-tition. This is easier to follow than it would be if broken after the *t*: part-ition.

The Apostrophe

The apostrophe is used to indicate either an omitted letter, or a possessive case. Here, the apostrophe is used to indicate a missing letter or letters:

> *It's* the wrong one. (Meaning: *It is* – the *i* is omitted)
> That *can't* be right. (Meaning: *cannot* – the *n* & *o* are omitted)
> *We'd* been to the coast. (Meaning: *We had* – the *h* & *a* are omitted)
> *You'll* be met at the station. (Meaning: *You will* – the *w* & *i* are omitted)

An apostrophe can be used to indicate ownership. In the singular case, the apostrophe is placed before the final *s*:

> That is Paul's car.
> The cat's bowl is empty.

When the plural form of a noun ends in *s*, then the possessive case is shown by an apostrophe *after* the final *s*:

> The cats' baskets were side by side.
> The houses' gardens were barren.

When plural nouns do not end in *s*, the possessive case is shown by an apostrophe *before* the *s*:

> The workmen's clothes were dirty.
> The women's party was noisy.

Note: *It's* should not be confused with *its*. *Its* is the possessive form of *it* and needs no apostrophe. *It's* is an abbreviation. For example:

It's a lovely day. (*It's* means: *It is*)
The car had its headlights on. (*its* means: *belonging to it*)

Brackets

Brackets, also known as parenthesis, are used to indicate a phrase which does not grammatically form part of a sentence:

The fine tolerances associated with precision engineering (discussed earlier) tend to result in high production costs.

Words placed in brackets can be removed from the sentence without altering the sense.

Brackets can be used to include asides not essential to the piece. That isn't to say words placed in brackets are *necessarily* unimportant, for at times they can convey essential information.

The Dash

The dash should not be confused with the hyphen; the two have completely different functions.

A dash is longer than a hyphen. A dash can be created on a typewriter by use of a double hyphen. Alternatively, in order to avoid confusion with a hyphen, a dash can be indicated by use of a hyphen with a space left on either side of it. For example: since - for.

A dash can be used to indicate a pause, particularly to create dramatic effect:

Paul could hardly stand - his legs were covered with blood.

A series of dashes is sometimes used to indicate a word has been censored, each dash indicating a missing letter:

'You b----- idiot!'

Dashes are sometimes used in place of brackets:

Joyce went next door (for the third time) to complain about the noise.
Joyce went next door – for the third time – to complain about the noise.

Quotation Marks

Quotation marks, or inverted commas, indicate direct speech. Either single or double inverted commas may be used to denote the actual words used:

'Wait a minute,' said George, 'you have forgotten your hat.'
"Wait a minute," said George, "you have forgotten your hat."

It is more common these days, for single inverted commas to be used, except when a quotation appears within a passage of direct speech:

'I was crossing Oxford Street when Mary Fox tapped me on the shoulder and said, "Where are you going?" I had no choice but to tell her.'

When a quotation continues for more than one paragraph, it is convention to open the inverted commas at the beginning of each paragraph but to close them only at the end of the last paragraph:

'You really must learn to relax. The arrangements have been made for long enough – everything has been checked and double-checked. Nothing can go wrong.
  'As for me, I'm going down to the cafe for something to eat. You won't see nerves get the better of me.'

Spelling

Whilst incorrect grammar can go unnoticed in a piece written in a stylish way, bad spelling cannot be overcome so easily. Bad spelling can instil hostile feelings in an editor and will reduce the chances of a sale.

In addition to creating a bad impression, incorrect spelling can change the sense of a piece of writing. To demonstrate what I mean, here are a few examples that have actually found their way into print:

> Mechanic required to carry out repairs to all makes of vehicles. Wages commiserate with ability.
>
> *Helston Free Gazette.*

This advertisement is hardly likely to draw enthusiastic replies for *commiserate* means to feel or express pity for. What the advertiser meant to say was: Wages *commensurate* with ability. *Commensurate* means proportionate.

Here is another example from the *Bucks Examiner*:

> Well-fitted kitchens (oven, hob & extractor hood, waist disposal unit).

I doubt this advertiser really wanted to dispose of part of a human body (*waist* being part of the human anatomy) but instead meant *waste* as in *refuse*.

Finally, from *Farmers Weekly* came this gem:

> Wanted – buried holly trees. Midlands area.

Whilst the roots of a holly tree no doubt grow beneath the earth (*buried*) it is likely the majority of it grows above ground. What this advertiser was looking for was trees bearing fruit: *berried*.

Just about everyone has been confused about the spelling of some words at some time or another. And this is hardly surprising when you consider how the English language came into being.

Spelling has evolved over around 800 years from different regional dialects into what is accepted as correct English today. Very often, words are not spelt the way they sound in speech, which gives rise to confusion. Whilst some rules can be developed to govern correct spelling, there are many exceptions to them. Take, for example, the rule that *i* comes before *e* except after *c*, when the sound is *ee*. This works well enough most of the time.

_i_ before _e_:
believe, fiend, grief, niece, piece, relieve, siege, thief.

except after _c_:
ceiling, conceit, conceive, deceive, perceive, receipt, receive.

But there are exceptions to the rule:
seize, weir, weird.

There are many words too, that contain *ie* or *ei* but do not have an *ee* sound. The rule *i* before *e* except after *c* cannot be applied to these words. For example:
eight, feint, heir, leisure, reign, sovereign, veil, vein, weight.

It is possible to learn all of these exceptions, of course, and how and why they are applied. This is fine for those interested enough to take the trouble, but for the majority of us there are so many rules and exceptions to the rules that it is easier to learn the spelling of individual words than it is to learn the rules governing them. A good English dictionary is therefore an essential tool of the writer's trade, as is a good thesaurus of synonyms and antonyms. *The Concise Oxford Dictionary* published by Oxford University Press is as good a dictionary as you will need, and a copy of one of the many versions of *Roget's Thesaurus* will serve you well.

A study of the following words will also help to improve your spelling.

Commonly Misspelled Words:
Absence, accelerate, acceptable, accommodate, accurate, achieve, acknowledge, acquaintance, acquire, across, address, aerial, aeroplane, agreeable, aisle, amount, anxious, appalling, appoint, argue, assistant, association, athlete, authorise, autumn, awkward, beautiful, beige, belief, benefit, benefited, bicycle, biscuit, build, business, cease, ceiling, changeable, chaos, cheque, chief, chimney, college, colourful, column, commit, conceit, condemn, conscience, conscious, criticism, deceive, decision, definitely, describe, desire, despair, desperate, develop, disappear, disappoint, disciple, dissatisfy, eccentric, eerie, efficient, embarrass, endeavour, exaggerate, exceed, except, excitement, exercise, existence, extremely, fascinate, feasible, February, financial, foreign, forty, fulfil, fulfilment, fulfilled, gauge, gorgeous, government, grammar, grief, grievance, handkerchief, height, holiday, humorous, humour, illegible, imaginary, immediately, immensely, incidentally, independent, indispensable, innocence, insistent, install, installation, interruption, irrelevant, irritable, its, jewellery, judge, knack, knock, knowledge, labour, laughter, leisure, library, likeable, loveable, manoeuvre, maintain, marriage, miscellaneous, mischievous, mistakable, mortgage, murmur, necessary, neighbour, niece, ninety, noticeable, occasionally, occur, occurred, occurrence, omission, panic, parallel, pastime, permissible, personal, personnel, philosophy, physician, possess, preliminary, prescribe, privilege, proceed, profession, psychiatrist, psychology, pursue, quay, questionnaire, queue, receive, receipt, recommend, relief, repetition, resource, restaurant, rhyme, rhythm, ridiculous, secretary, scene, scenery, schedule, seize, separate, similar, sincere, skilful, solemn, sophisticated, souvenir, stationary, stationery, succeed, successful, sufficient, supersede, surprise, suppress, temporary, theatre, thorough, tongue, transfer, typical, tyre, umbrella, unnecessary,

unnoticed, until, vague, vegetable, vicious, view, Wednesday, weight, weird, whole, wilful, woollen, wreck, yacht, yeast, yield, zodiac.

Same Sound – Different Meaning:

All	Awl
Allowed	Aloud
Altar	Alter
Ascent	Assent
Bail	Bale
Balmy	Barmy
Bare	Bear
Beach	Beech
Board	Bored
Boarder	Border
Bough	Bow
Boy	Buoy
Brake	Break
Bread	Bred
Buy	By
Canon	Cannon
Cellar	Seller
Cheque	Check
Chord	Cord
Coarse	Course
Compliment	Complement
Corps	Corpse
Council	Counsel
Currant	Current
Cymbal	Symbol
Dear	Deer
Dependant	Dependent
Descendant	Descendent
Die	Dye

Draft	Draught
Dual	Duel
Faint	Feint
Fair	Fare
Farther	Father
Fate	Fête
Flair	Flare
For	Four
Forbear	Forebear
Forego	Forgo
Formally	Formerly
Freeze	Frieze
Gage	Gauge
Gilt	Guilt
Gorilla	Guerrilla
Hair	Hare
Hall	Haul
Hear	Here
Him	Hymn
Hoard	Horde
Holy	Wholly
Hoarse	Horse
Idle	Idol
Incite	Insight
Isle	Aisle
Its	It's
Kernel	Colonel
Key	Quay
Knew	New
Know	No
Leak	Leek
Lessen	Lesson
Licence	License
Lightening	Lightning
Load	Lode

Loan	Lone	
Maize	Maze	
Mare	Mayor	
Meat	Meet	
Medal	Meddle	
Metal	Mettle	
Mews	Muse	
Moor	More	
Oral	Aural	
Packed	Pact	
Pain	Pane	
Pail	Pale	
Pair	Pear	Pare
Passed	Past	
Pause	Paws	
Peace	Piece	
Peal	Peel	
Peak	Pique	
Pedal	Peddle	
Peer	Pier	
Practice	Practise	
Presence	Presents	
Principal	Principle	
Queue	Cue	
Quire	Choir	
Rain	Reign	Rein
Raise	Raze	
Red	Read	
Read	Reed	
Right	Rite	
Role	Roll	
Scent	Sent	
Sew	So	Sow
Serial	Cereal	
Sight	Site	Cite

Stair	Stare	
Stake	Steak	
Steal	Steel	
Stationary	Stationery	
Stile	Style	
Storey	Story	
Straight	Strait	
Symbol	Cymbal	
Tale	Tail	
Taught	Taut	
Their	There	
Through	Threw	
To	Too	Two
Troop	Troupe	
Vain	Vane	Vein
Waist	Waste	
Wait	Weight	
Waive	Wave	
Ware	Wear	Where
Weather	Whether	
Whole	Hole	
Which	Witch	
Wright	Right	Rite
Yoke	Yolk	

Similar Sound – Different Meaning:

Accept	Except
Access	Excess
Adapt	Adopt
Advice	Advise
Affect	Effect
Alley	Ally
Amiable	Amenable
Angel	Angle

Apposite	Opposite
Assurance	Insurance
Breath	Breathe
Censor	Censure
Conceive	Concede
Conscience	Conscious
Continual	Continuous
Co-respondent	Correspondent
Defer	Differ
Deprecate	Depreciate
Deride	Derive
Desert	Dessert
Device	Devise
Diagram	Diaphragm
Dilate	Dilute
Elicit	Illicit
Elusive	Illusive
Emigrate	Immigrate
Eminent	Imminent
Envelop	Envelope
Exercise	Exorcise
Final	Finale
Funereal	Funeral
Gamble	Gambol
Genteel	Gentle
Grisly	Grizzly
Human	Humane
Hypercritical	Hypocritical
Illusion	Allusion
Immunity	Impunity
Incredible	Incredulous
Ingenious	Ingenuous
Insure	Ensure
Juggler	Jugular
Later	Latter

51

Lay	Lie
Loath	Loathe
Loose	Lose
Magnate	Magnet
Moral	Morale
Notable	Notorious
Official	Officious
Oldest	Eldest
Partition	Petition
Personal	Personnel
Physic	Psychic
Practicable	Practical
Prescribe	Proscribe
Prophecy	Prophesy
Raise	Rise
Report	Rapport
Recent	Resent
Reverend	Reverent
Sensual	Sensuous
Sceptic	Septic
Sever	Severe
Statue	Statute
Suit	Suite
Treaties	Treatise
Uninterested	Disinterested
Unorganised	Disorganised
Veracious	Voracious
Were	Where

British and American Spelling

There are many differences in spelling between British English and American English. Some English publishers prefer the use of British English and some prefer American English. Publishers distributing their wares on both sides of the Atlantic often prefer the use of American English. It is therefore as well to check the house style of your target market before deciding which to use. But if in doubt, use British English; your spelling can always be corrected at copy editing stage.

Here are the main differences between British and American spellings:

British:	American:
Aeroplane	Airplane
Aluminium	Aluminum
Axe	Ax
Centre	Center
Cheque	Check
Colour	Color
Defence	Defense
Dived	Dove
Enrol	Enroll
Enthral	Enthrall
Fulfil	Fulfill
Grey	Gray
Gaol, Jail	Jail
Honour	Honor
Jewellery	Jewelry
Kerb	Curb
Labour	Labor
Levelled	Leveled
Meagre	Meager
Nett, Net	Net
Offence	Offense
Plough	Plow
Pretence	Pretense
Programme	Program
Pyjamas	Pajamas
Sceptic	Skeptic
Skilful	Skillful

Storey	Story
Through	Thru
Tyre	Tire
Wagon, Waggon	Waggon
Woollen	Woolen

3

Some Legalities

Copyright

International copyright law is a complicated issue but one which demands some of your attention if you are to be an author. Having said that, an in depth understanding of copyright as it affects us in Britain isn't usually necessary for the majority of aspiring writers who are about to embark on their career. I'll therefore try to keep this section as straightforward as possible in an endeavour not to send you to sleep.

Regulations covering copyright vary throughout the world but in the United Kingdom we are governed by The Copyright, Design and Patents Act of 1988. This act changed the existing Copyright Act of 1956 and came into effect on 1st August 1989. Much of the 1956 Act has been restated but some fundamental moral rights were introduced, which we'll get to in a moment.

Essentially, the Copyright Act prevents the copying of the written word, music, television, films, sound recordings, and other literary works as well as all manner of artistic works such as paintings, drawings, charts, maps, sculptures, brass rubbings and the like. As for this review, we'll stick to those points most relevant to the writer.

A written work has to be original to be afforded protection of copyright and it has to have some substance. It is automatically protected provided it is of sufficient length to have involved the author in a certain amount of intellectual endeavour.

Copyright only exists in a work once it has been recorded in writing or otherwise (on audio tape or video, for example). It is therefore important to get finalised thoughts recorded onto paper or by other means at the earliest moment. Once this has been done, the form of the words is your copyright. In other words, all written works are copyright irrespective of whether or not they have been published. A work becomes copyright as soon as it has been written and it applies to all works.

There is a quirk in the Copyright Act as far as letters are concerned. A letter itself (the piece of paper and its ink) belongs to the recipient, but the copyright in it belongs to the writer. The copyright in the composition is afforded the same protection as other written works.

Many aspiring writers ask the question: 'I have had this brilliant idea for a novel. How can I prevent it from being stolen?' I'm afraid the short answer to this is: you can't. There is no copyright in an idea – only the way that idea is expressed. You will therefore be wise to write out your ideas into their final design or, alternatively, produce them in sufficient body to have form. When you express an idea in writing it is automatically copyright.

To labour the point, the law of copyright protects the form of a work and not the idea behind the form. Titles of books, magazines and songs are not protected by copyright because they are too short to be regarded as literary works. In short, if you want to be sure your work is copyrightable ensure it is long enough to form a complete composition.

The 1988 Copyright Act introduced certain moral rights. The main points of these rights are:

- **The right of paternity**. This is the right of the author to be identified whenever a work is published, performed or broadcast. However, the author does not benefit from paternity unless he or she asserts that right in writing. Also, it is not a right in a work which has its copyright vested in the author's employer.

- **The right of integrity.** This is the right of the author to object to 'derogatory treatment' of a work. The term 'treatment' means the adding to, deletion from, alteration or adaption of a piece of work which distorts or mutilates it to the detriment of the author's reputation. A 'derogatory treatment' is one which amounts to 'distortion or mutilation' or is 'otherwise prejudicial to the honour or reputation of the author'. This doesn't apply to normal editing, only to changes which distort or mutilate the work.

- **The right to object to false attribution.** This is the right not to have a work falsely attributed to you. This could be considered to be the opposite of the right of paternity. One way this can work is to prevent a publisher wrongly identifying someone famous as the author of a book in an endeavour to improve sales.

- **The right of privacy.** If you had taken some holiday snaps for your private use and suddenly you became famous (that is, if you weren't already famous) you have the right not to have those pictures published or exhibited in public.

The rights of paternity and integrity do not apply when work appears in a periodical such as a newspaper or a magazine, nor do they apply to collections such as dictionaries, encyclopaedias and yearbooks. You may therefore wish to specify that no changes may be made in your contributions without your consent. You may also wish to ask for confirmation that your name will appear as the author on your articles and short stories.

Moral rights can be waived by written agreement or with the consent of the author, but they cannot be assigned to someone else.

No formalities need to be observed in order to copyright an original written work. The work does not have to be printed nor to be published to receive the benefit of protection. It doesn't have to be registered, nor does any notice of any kind have to be displayed on the work. Copyright is yours from the moment you set pen to paper or speak into your recorder. (This is not the case in some other countries, including the United States of America.) So, just because the word 'copyright' or the symbol © may not appear against a composition, it doesn't mean you can go ahead and copy to your heart's content. And just because something is old and out of print don't assume it is no longer protected (more about this in a moment).

Whilst no formalities are required to protect a work, it is wise to establish evidence of its date of completion, particularly if it is likely to be some time before it is to be published in commercial form. There are a couple of simple methods to achieve this. You could deposit a copy of your manuscript at a bank and obtain a dated receipt. This way, if there was ever any dispute as to the originator of the work you could demonstrate when yours was written. Alternatively, you could post a copy of your manuscript in a sealed envelope to yourself, only to be opened in the event of any dispute. This way the post mark would establish the date your work was written.

The duration of copyright protection varies throughout the world, but in an endeavour to rationalise this period throughout the countries of the EEC, Directive 93/98 was issued to make them all the same. This was introduced to fall into line with the community's highest figure (Germany) to provide a common standard. This modification took effect from 1st January 1996. Copyright now lasts 70 years from the end of the year in which the author died, where previously it was 50 years. For a work of joint authorship the period of protection runs from the end of the calendar year in which the last author died.

The revised copyright period of 70 years is retrospective.

The additional twenty years granted to existing copyright will belong to the owner of the copyright on 31st December 1995. Any copyright licence in existence, such as in a publishing contract, which is for the duration of copyright, continues to apply to the extended period, unless there has been an agreement to the contrary. For works published during the author's lifetime, the period of copyright begins from the date of publication. Where copyright has expired after 50 years, it will be restored if the author died within 70 years of 1st January 1996. For works where the identity of the author is unknown and which were created before 1st January 1996, the copyright will last until 50 years from when the work was written unless, during that time, it is made available to the public in which case it will be protected until 50 years from when it was first made available.

Copyright works may be sold by their owners to anyone who may wish to buy them. Sale of copyright is known as assignment. Alternatively, the copyright owner may grant a licence to someone else to exploit certain rights, whilst retaining the overall copyright. An assignment must be in writing and signed on behalf of the assignor. This assignment may be a simple exchange of letters; a more formal agreement is not usually considered necessary.

Licences often grant different rights to different parties. It is possible for a book-length work to assign hardback rights to one party and paperback rights to another. The foreign language rights could also be sold to another party and the film and the television rights to yet another.

Plagiarism

Plagiarism is the copying, or paraphrasing, of another author's work without acknowledgement or permission, unless the copyright has expired.

New authors often ask if their writing can be stolen. The short answer to this is: yes, it can, and sometimes it is. Cases of plagiarism coming to court are still relatively rare but they do occur. For example, damages were awarded against Julie Burchill and Times Newspapers for use of material from a book by Johnny Rogan.

More dramatically, Regine Deforges and her publisher were ordered to pay two million francs (£200,000) to the heirs of Margaret Mitchell for the plagiarism of *Gone With the Wind* in Deforges's novel *The Blue Bicycle*.

Clearly, plagiarism does occur but it is perhaps wise to remember that it doesn't occur as frequently as some beginning writers may fear.

It is an infringement of copyright to quote 'a substantial part' of a copyright work without permission. Unfortunately, the Copyright Act does not define what constitutes 'a substantial part'. When making a judgement on what constitutes 'a substantial part' the quality of the part as well as its length must be taken into account. 'Substantial' really means *important* rather than large.

So, if it is an infringement to copy other people's work, how do you gather facts to write about? For as Mark Twain once said: 'Adam was the only man who, when he said a good thing, knew that nobody had said it before him.' In today's times one could be excused for thinking that there is nothing new under the sun. But facts and ideas are not copyright, just the form in which they are expressed. There is nothing wrong in research.

Most areas of freelance writing involve the author in research at some stage or another. The storyteller will have to read up on the effects of different poisons if he or she is to have the criminal commit murder by this method. And the writer of the business column will often have to research facts and figures for use in articles. Research is a necessary part of a writer's life. It is perfectly legitimate provided it is undertaken in a proper manner. There is a maxim in writing circles which says: 'If you copy from one source you will be guilty of plagiarism. If you copy from several sources you will be undertaking legitimate research.' Well, this isn't strictly accurate, but it does give some indication of how research should be undertaken. You must record only the facts when rummaging through your source material, never the actual words used by others. Having said that, it is all too easy to unconsciously recall what you have read and to paraphrase it in your own writing. But you must avoid falling into this trap for otherwise you could very well be accused of plagiarism. All it takes is a little care.

We are not born with our knowledge, we acquire it from life experience and from what we are taught and learn from study. Very often, we acquire knowledge by reading. We do not copy the actual words written, simply the knowledge contained within those words. This is how to undertake research.

Basic plots are not copyright. This was demonstrated admirably by Georges Polti when he put together his much revered book *The Thirty-Six Dramatic Situations*. As the title suggests this book illustrates that all modern plots are but variations and adaptions of just 36 original situations. They are derived from what are said to be the *only* 36 human emotional conflicts to be experienced in life. Attempts have been made to disprove this theory but I am unaware of anyone who has come close to success. The book therefore demonstrates admirably that with just 36 basic plots to be had, in fiction at least, there are no new themes under the sun – simply the way they are expressed. But do bear in mind that if one of your plots is *very* similar to another author's, containing the same characters and the same sequence of events, you could well be accused of stealing some original thought. In such circumstances you could be guilty of plagiarism. The only defence in these circumstances would be to prove that you were totally unaware of the original book, which you would find very difficult to do.

There are a number of exceptions to the rules of infringement of copyright. These include: fair dealing with literary, dramatic, musical or artistic works for the purpose of research or private study, and fair dealing for the purpose of criticism or review.

If you do infringe copyright an injunction can be sought to prevent you continuing the infringement. Damages can be sought and if the action was successful, you would have to pay up. Usually, the amount you would have to pay would be what the copyright owner would have been likely to receive had a licence been granted.

Quotation for the 'purpose of criticism or review' is covered by 'fair dealing'. If the quotation is regarded as 'fair dealing' you need not seek permission to use it, but you must acknowledge the title and the author you have quoted. The Copyright Act gives no indication of how many words can be quoted under the 'fair dealing' rule. Each case must be judged on its merits. As we have said before, the amount quoted in relation to the remainder of the work will have a bearing. You have to exercise your own judgement as to what can be considered to be 'fair dealing'. In one case, four lines from a thirty-two line poem were deemed to amount to 'a substantial part'. In another case a film company infringed copyright by using just 20 seconds of a four minute tune without permission. It wasn't the time element that was important here but what was considered to be a 'substantial part' of the overall work.

The Society of Authors and The Publishers Association at one time stated that: 'they would usually regard as "fair dealing" the use of a single extract of up to 400 words, or a series of extracts (of which none exceeds 300 words) to a total of 800 words from a prose work, or of extracts to a total of 40 lines from a poem, provided that this did not exceed a quarter of a poem. Of course, the words must be quoted in the context of "criticism or review".' This is of course only a guide and each case must be judged on its merits, as we have already said.

Where illustrations are to be used, permission is always required. And it is worth repeating that permissions are always needed when quotations fall outside of what can be considered to be 'fair dealing'. It should also be noted that permission is needed for *all* quoted material for anthologies no matter how short they may be.

If you are to write a work under contract it is usual for contracts to specify it to be the author's responsibility to obtain, and to pay for, all necessary permissions to use long quotations or illustrations. Under these circumstances, you must clear with the publisher which territory the permissions need to cover: British Commonwealth, USA, the world, etc. Once this has been established you should write to the copyright holder for permission to quote from the work. In the first instance, write to the publisher for permission. If the publisher does not control the rights, it will forward your enquiry to whoever does, often the author.

When applying for permission outline in what context it will be used, for this will have a bearing on its value and what fee is to be charged.

To sum up; the best approach to steer clear of plagiarism is to try to avoid the need to copy anything. If you do find the need to copy or quote, either ensure it is within the confines of 'fair dealing' or get written permission from the copyright holder first.

Passing off

There is no copyright in a title, but you should avoid using one which is already well known, otherwise you are in danger of being accused of 'passing off'. If you were to call your book *Rich Man, Poor Man* for example, you could be accused of 'passing off'. In this example, 'passing off' would be to mislead potential readers into the belief that your book was written by the author of the original novel, Irwin Shaw. You shouldn't use a title that has already been used before if it is likely to cause confusion as to whose work it is.

Two books having the same title won't always cause such confusion, of course. Take Mickey Spillane's thriller set in New York entitled *The Deep*. In this case, *The Deep* referred to the theme character where *Deep* was his name. Some years later another, totally different, novel having the same title appeared. In this one the title referred to the ocean. Did the second novel confuse book buyers over which book it was they were buying? Well, no it didn't – the two books were marketed years apart, they had quite different jacket designs, and they were on totally different themes. There was no similarity at all and no confusion could have arisen.

Similarly, there is no copyright in an author's name – but the same warning on 'passing off' applies. If your name happens to be Harold Robbins you could be in a spot of bother should you wish to write steamy novels. You would be in grave danger of being accused of passing your work off as the work of the already famous author.

In the same vein, if an author's *pen name* is also used by another writer which may lead people to think your work was written by that of the other author, you could be accused of 'passing off'.

Care also has to be exercised that you do not infringe the Trade Descriptions Act. In 1991 a case was brought against Harper-Collins after they published two books billing them as Alistair MacLean's *Night Watch* and Alistair MacLean's *Death Train*. The action was brought because these books had not been written by thriller writer Alistair MacLean, but had been written after his death by another writer with the similar name of Alistair MacNeill. Both novels were based on storylines and character studies supplied by plots which Alistair MacLean had outlined before his death. These books had been written with the agreement of Alistair MacLean's literary executors. The case was brought as in contravention of the Trade Descriptions Act by indicating that they were written by Alistair MacLean when they were not. The case hinged around the use of an apostrophe in the two books' titles which utilised a script identical to the author's original which made it appear as though the books were written by the bestselling author himself. Alistair MacNeill's name had appeared in much smaller type at the bottom of the cover, where Alistair MacLean's was in bold type at the top. It was held that these books were not up to the standard of Alistair MacLean and that the author Alistair MacNeill had never had books published before. The case was brought by Warwickshire Trading

Standards Department following three complaints by people who had read the books mistakenly thinking that they had been written by Alistair MacLean. HarperCollins were found guilty and fined £6,250 with £4,151 costs for selling books under a misleading title.

A similar situation arose when Raymond Chandler, who died in 1959, left behind an incomplete manuscript. Here, Chandler's story *The Poodle Springs Story* was completed by Robert B. Parker and billed simply as *Poodle Springs*. The publishers, Futura, handled their version in a somewhat different way to the HarperCollins novels. The Futura book gave both authors the same prominence on the front cover with their names in identical character size and style. On top of this the cover also carried, albeit in small lettering, an Ed McBain quote: 'A rattling good thriller . . . At his very best, Parker sounds more like Chandler than Chandler himself.' In this case there could be little doubt that the book was written by both Parker and Chandler and so there was no danger of a potential reader being in doubt about who wrote it.

Libel

The law of libel is made up partly of common law (the law made by judges) and partly of the Defamation Act 1952.

The Penguin English Dictionary defines libel as a: 'written or printed statement likely to damage a person's reputation; act of publishing such a statement; harmful misrepresentation; untrue and harmful remark.' Let's expand this further by quoting *Fraser on Libel and Slander, 7th Edition*. Libel is: 'a statement concerning any person which exposes him to hatred, ridicule or contempt, or which causes him to be shunned or avoided, or which has a tendency to injure him in his office, profession or trade.'

To be libellous, defamation must be expressed in permanent form, such as in writing, on film or video, on television or radio.

Few writers are intentionally libellous, of course. It is in an aspiring writer's interest not to be so, for more reasons than mere damage to personal finance. If there is a hint of a suspicion that your criticism of somebody is in any way libellous it is doubtful any publisher would touch it. Hardly an action required if you want to see yourself in print.

When writing about real people you need to ask yourself if you would like it if someone wrote the same thing about you. If you would not, make absolutely certain of your 'facts' before committing them to print.

Occasionally though, hatred can run so deep that someone will make a *deliberate* defamatory statement in permanent form. In this case the defamation is classed as criminal libel. Needless to say, cases of criminal libel coming to court are rare. If anyone were foolish enough to commit such an act they must know that they are likely to be on the losing end of legal action.

There is a maxim in writing circles which says you should write about what you know. This is sound advice for it will give your writing the feel of authority, but be wary when it comes to creating characters for your fiction. If you base your characters on living people you are bound to be in danger of libelling them. Your characters must be sufficiently removed from real people so that readers cannot connect the two. If you were to use as one of your characters a description of a real living person, it would be poor protection to simply change his or her name. Also, you should make all reasonable checks that your fictional characters' names do not correspond with living persons. A disclaimer at the front of a novel which says: 'All characters in this book are entirely imaginary and any resemblance to persons living or dead, or actual events, is purely coincidental', will have little protecting effect if you have indeed libelled a real person.

A libel action must be started within three years of publication, otherwise it becomes time-barred.

There are five defences to a libel action. These are:

- **Justification**. A statement of truth cannot be libellous. The *Concise Oxford Dictionary* defines 'defame' as to 'attack the good reputation of, speak ill of'. Just because a statement is defamatory it does not necessarily mean it isn't true. But if you write about someone in these circumstances you would need to be sure of your ground and be able to prove that your statement was true. You would need to be *very* sure of what you considered to be your 'facts'. Otherwise you could be put to a great deal of trouble and expense in court.

- **Fair comment**. This is a defence if you can demonstrate that the words in question were fair comment on a matter of public interest. Matters of opinion on literary works, for example, can be scathing but still be held to be fair comment. Fair comment is an expression of genuinely held opinion that is clearly not expressed as a statement of fact. Such comment would allow the reader to agree or disagree with it.

- **Privilege**. There are certain occasions which are 'privileged' and where defamatory statements do not incur liability. These cover such things as the reporting of public meetings. In general, newcomers to writing are unlikely to be too concerned with this area of legislation.

- **Innocent defamation**. It is, of course, foolish to write something you know to be libellous, but you also need to be alert to the possibility of being unwittingly guilty of libel. Let's say a real dignitary living in the town where you have set your novel has the same name as one of your characters who is a thoroughly disreputable rogue. You could find yourself in trouble under such circumstances. But all you can do is to take reasonable precautions to ensure such errors don't happen. Research the town of this rogue to ensure such a coincidence can't happen. At least look through the telephone directory covering the home town to ensure there is no-one there having the same name. If your words are in fact libellous, but you had no intention of being libellous, you can make an 'offer of amends'. Should this be accepted all that would usually be required of you is to publish an apology and pay costs. If, however, your offer wasn't accepted, and the offended party instigated proceedings, your offer would provide you with a good defence in court. But be careful, anything defamatory is presumed untrue unless you can show otherwise.

● **Apology.** This defence only applies to libels in newspapers and periodicals. In these cases it is a defence that the libel was made without malice and without gross negligence and that before an action was commenced, or as soon afterwards as possible, a full apology was inserted in the same publication.

Civil claims for libel cannot be brought on behalf of the dead, for it is held that the dead *cannot* be libelled. But beware you do not make derogatory remarks about a dead person which may adversely affect the reputation of his or her descendants. You have to be careful about any implications for the living. If, for example, you described a woman as a prostitute and a drug taker, her husband may be able to demonstrate that his reputation as a widower had suffered. Having said that, cases of such a nature being brought are rare. As a rule of thumb, the more distant someone's death the less chance you have of upsetting the living should you write about it.

Awards for defamation can be extremely damaging to the bank balance. At least in America. According to *The Guinness Book of Records 1996*: 'The record award in a libel case is $58 million, to Vic Feazell, a former district attorney, on 20 April 1991 at Waco, Texas, USA. He claimed that he had been libelled by a Dallas-based television station and one of its reporters in 1985, and that this had ruined his reputation. The parties reached a settlement on 29 June 1991, but neither side would disclose the amount.'

Clearly, the best bet when writing about living people is to be nice. But if you must write about a sensitive area, ensure accuracy.

4

Presentation

Hand-written work

In the main, freelance submissions to newspaper and magazine editors, not to mention book publishers, will need to be typewritten if they are to be given any serious consideration. Hand-written manuscripts may have been perfectly acceptable in the days of Jane Austen and Elizabeth Barrett Browning, but not today. In our modern high-tech world, magazine submissions have to be high-tech presented if they are to match editorial expectations. But there are exceptions. Not many, I'll grant you, but there are some, which we can take a look at now.

Letters to the Editor
Pick up any magazine or newspaper and you are likely to find a feature devoted to readers' letters. Their subject-matter and level of literacy vary according to the subject covered and to the target readership. But most will have one thing in common: they will have been hand-written.

Those who write to magazines rarely take the trouble to type their offerings. The pen is good enough for such occasions. And that includes people who aspire to greater heights. Many aspiring freelance scribes embark on a writing career by specialising in letters to the editor. Letters can provide an excellent second income.

In the majority of cases it is a good idea *not* to type a reader's letter. A typewritten letter can look as though it is the work of a professional; of someone who writes for money rather than someone who is simply an avid reader. If you want to make a sale at this level it is wise to appear to be a regular buyer of the magazine.

This isn't true of all markets, of course. Some up-market periodicals would find nothing strange in their readers owning either a typewriter or a word processor, or indeed, to be able to utilise secretarial services for their personal correspondence. But these magazines are the exception rather than the rule, and in general letters should be neatly hand-written. It is all a question of analysing the market and making judgement.

If you do decide to type your letter, lay it out in the manner described for hand-written submissions which follows.

Hand-written letters, particularly those to editors, should be easy to read. But this is not always how they appear.

In days gone by, I used to edit a small press magazine entitled *Mosaic*. This was specifically aimed at aspiring writers, but despite the advice we gave on proper presentation, subscribers would still write to us in a scrawl that not even MI5's decoding department would be able to decipher. With the best will in the world such contributions would never find their way into print. If you are going to hand-write your letters you need to ensure they are as well-presented as you can possibly make them. Editors are busy people and will soon pass over a scrawl in favour of a contribution that is easy to read.

Having said that, if there is any danger at all that your handwriting would be unclear to anyone, *print* your address at the top of your letter. Road names, towns and sometimes counties can be alien to the reader. Short of pulling out an atlas no-one could be sure they have the right spelling. So, make it impossible for anyone to make a mistake. Print your address clearly. You don't have to use block capitals – lower case is fine so long as it is perfectly clear.

It is always best to add your telephone number after your address, in case of any editorial query. Remember, editors receive a great many readers' letters, so make it easy for them to contact you if they need to, otherwise your letter may be passed over in favour of the next letter in the pile.

Always try to address your letter personally to the editor using his or her name. It will nearly always be given in the magazine. Sometimes, the letters editor will be different from the editor-in-chief, so ensure you address it to the right person. If no editor's name is mentioned in the letter feature, look at the credits page at the front of the magazine to see if it is printed there. If you cannot find the editor's name anywhere in the magazine address your letter 'Dear Editor'. This is much friendlier than 'Dear Sir or Madam'.

The next thing to decide about your layout is whether or not to use a heading to your letter. A good many magazines use either individual or group headings to letters. Usually, this is done simply to liven up the page. Examine your target publication to see how they handle their letters. If they use headings, it may be worthwhile adding one to yours. I know editors usually make up these things for themselves but if you have taken the trouble to compose one it at least shows you know the style of the magazine. And it could save the editor the trouble of making one up. Ensure yours is clearly a heading and not part of your letter by using either capitals or lower case underlined.

When you come to the body of your letter ensure it is not too long or too short. Examine what has been used before and follow that example. Watch sentence and paragraph length. Popular periodicals often use short ones.

When you come to sign off, be honest about your signature. Is it legible? Most aren't. If yours is an indecipherable squiggle, print your name beneath.

An example of a reader's letter is given in *Fig 2*.

Some people do not want the whole world to know they write. The road digger simply may not wish his co-workers to be aware

3 Inkwell Street,
Story Town,
Blottinghamshire,
TT2 6XZ.

Tel: 1111 22222.
9th May 1996.

Dear Editor,

Vegetable Rain?

I was in the garden with my two year old daughter the other day when she pointed into the sky and said, "There's a white cabbage up there."

With a mental picture of garden produce flying through the air, I followed her finger to find she was looking at a cabbage white butterfly!

Yours sincerely,

A. Writer

M. WRITER

Fig 2. Typical presentation of a reader's letter

that he writes about knitting patterns to a woman's magazine in his spare time. Or the florist may not wish her customers to know that she takes up the position of anchor in her local tug-of-war team at weekends. There are also those avid letters writers who write so often that they submit regularly to the same market. They don't want to miss the chance of more than one sale so how do they get over the fact that editors are unlikely to print more than one of their letters at once? The answer is simple: don't use your real name. Use several others instead. There is no difficulty in using a *nom de plume*. You simply pick one that suits you. But if you submit to paying markets, beware. Payments for published letters will usually be in the form of crossed cheques. These can only be paid into the account of the payee. So use only names of friends and relatives with whom you can come to an arrangement to pay into their account in exchange for cash. Perhaps in return for the small bribe of allowing them to read your research magazines. The names on payment cheques can be a real headache if you don't make provision for them, so make arrangements before you write.

Today, a good many photographs are printed alongside readers' letters. Gossip weeklies are often extremely visual and the trend for publishing submitted snapshots by readers is on the increase. This is in some measure due to reader demand for their magazines to be a 'quick read', but it is more about the ability of modern printing technology to take the reproduction of colour illustrations in its stride. Letter writers should take heed of this trend when researching markets. If your target outlet uses photographs, you should follow suit. You don't need to be David Bailey to take reproducible snapshots these days. Don't worry too much about which type of film to use or what size of print to send in. Most mass-market magazines can cope with just about anything thrown at them today. This is not necessarily true of 'artwork' which accompanies articles and books, but for readers' letters they are fine. (We'll come to 'artwork' later.) Even those magazines using only black and white illustrations can use colour prints as their base. Avoid sending in transparencies though, for despite advancing technology not all outlets have yet learned to cope with them.

Always keep a copy of what you send out, for ideas are valuable. If a submission doesn't find editorial favour first time out you can always rewrite it to suit another market.

Cuttings
Many magazines carry a feature reproducing misprints sent in by their readers. These items are merely extracts from other publications which have made an error in typesetting to produce an unscheduled comic effect. Simply cut out the misprint, stick it onto a postcard and address it to your chosen market. Don't forget to add your own name and address, too. This may seem obvious but editors really do receive postcards without them. What a pity it would be to miss out on an acceptance cheque for such a simple oversight.

Other Hand-Written Submissions
Sometimes verse, limericks and jokes feature among the readers' contributions slot. These can be submitted in the form of a readers' letter.

There are two other occasions when you may just get away with hand-written submissions.

Many small presses today produce magazines and newsletters from the energies of just one or two people. These publications vary in quality from dog-eared photocopies to professional-looking glossies. Content also varies from the first attempts of L-plate authors to semi-professional literature. Their circulation figures can be less than a hundred copies up to a couple of thousand or so. Rates of pay for contributions vary from just a free copy of the magazine in which work appears to a few pounds per thousand words. Another thing which varies is the attitude of editors. Some will accept hand-written work whereas others won't. And you cannot always tell which are which simply by the look of them. Some of the moth-eaten ones will, surprisingly, stipulate that they will only consider typewritten work whereas some very posh small press magazines will consider hand-written submissions. And, of course, sometimes the reverse is true, too. So, you need to examine what the editorial says. If no statement is made, and you want to submit hand-written work, you had best enquire first.

The other occasion where hand-written submissions are sometimes accepted is when the nationals invite reader-written submissions. These are usually articles (particularly personal experience pieces) or sometimes short stories. Whatever is being sought will usually be spelt out by publication in question. It will give the type of item, perhaps the style (particularly when inviting first person pieces), the length, and whether any editorial help is offered. Often, these blurbs will also advise whether *clearly* hand-written submissions will be considered. If no such statement is made you would do well not to try it. You had best play safe and type your submission. But even when hand-written work is considered it is best to submit these in manuscript format unless a particular layout has been specified.

And, as always, keep a copy.

The Typescript

Apart from those exceptions outlined above, all manuscripts which are to be offered for publication should be neatly typed if they are to be given any serious consideration. They should be typed on one side only of good quality A4 white bond paper having a minimum weight of 80gsm (grams per square metre).

If possible don't use a fancy typeface. Those that look like handwriting for example, won't find editorial favour. Use a plain face such as Times New Roman in 10 or 12 point. Type only in this style; use no bold or italics. If you wish to have italics in your finished copy, underline those words you want to see italicised. This is the convention which tells the typesetter to do it.

Typewriter (or printer) ribbons should be black and preferably of the type that can be used once only. All copy should be crisp and clear. If you have to use a cotton or nylon ribbon, don't be tempted to double up on its use so that it produces only pale, insipid print.

If you use a typewriter and you make a mistake, use a correction fluid or correction paper, never x-out your mistakes. If you slip in too many typos, scrap the page and start again.

Throughout your typescript be consistent in its presentation. If you begin by quoting metric measurements on page one, don't switch to old fashioned imperial units later on. If your fictional characters make use of single quotation marks in their opening remarks don't have them use double quotation marks part way through. But note that these days single quote marks are nearly always used for speech in fiction. Double quotation marks are usually restricted to quotes within speech. If you date an event as 11th May 1996 at the beginning of your manuscript, don't switch to another form later on and quote a date of June 14th, 1996. Be consistent all the way through.

Adopt a uniform approach to numbers. It is usual for numbers under 10 to be spelled out (eg: eight), whereas numbers of 10 and above are written in numerals. The exception to this is when beginning a sentence with a number when it should always be spelled out.

Remember too, that these days abbreviations are usually written without full-stops, as in: BBC, MP and USA.

Keep headings consistent. A good approach is to use capital letters for headings and lower case with capitals at the beginning of words for sub-headings. If you wish to employ more than two levels of heading (which would be unusual) indicate each level by identifying them in the margin in some way, such as 1 for the highest level, 2 for the next, and so on.

When your piece is finished, check it thoroughly for grammatical and spelling errors. Nothing is designed to alienate an editor faster than bad spelling.

The majority of editors prefer to have no fixings to manuscripts. No pins, no staples, no treasury tags. At most use a paper clip for short works. For book-length manuscripts use nothing at all; just the box you transport it in.

Now let us take a look at what various manuscripts should look like. But be warned: there is no accepted standard for manuscript presentation. Works have been written on the subject from time to time but, as I write this, there is no British Standard or Code of Practice outlining how they should be laid out. Different editors therefore have differing ideas on how the finer details should be handled. Nevertheless, if you follow some basic rules which have been established by tradition over the years no editor should have too much cause for complaint so long as it is clear and neat. If work looks professional it will tend to give the impression the writer will have a similarly professional approach when determining what the publisher is likely to require in terms of content, style and length. Editors will certainly give such submissions priority over tatty ones, in the hope of finding something appropriate and therefore usable. A manuscript is the best introduction an author can have. You wouldn't go to a job interview at a bank in a boiler suit; treat your manuscript in the same way and you are on your way to making a sale.

Articles

The first page of the manuscript should comprise a cover sheet outlining what the work is, what it is about and whose efforts have produced it. Let's imagine we're typing one up.

In the upper right hand corner type your name and address. Use your *real* name, not any *nom de plume* you choose to write under. This is to enable the cheque to be made out to you so that you can bank it without difficulty when your work is accepted. Your address should be your full postal address, including postcode, to enable that cheque to be safely posted to you.

Below your address, type your telephone number so that the

editorial team can reach you if need be, for all of the reasons that we outlined for hand-written work.

Do not date your manuscript. The date can be included in your cover letter, which we'll come to in the next chapter.

The remainder of the cover sheet should be centred.

Scroll down nine spaces and type, in upper case, the title of your article. (This title will be used for identification purposes if your work is accepted for publication. However, editors often change a title at editing stage. This can be due to space limitations, or simply because their own chosen one is more in keeping with their image.)

Scroll down nine spaces and type, in lower case: 'An article by'. Beneath this type your name or *nom de plume*.

Scroll down nine spaces and type, in lower case, your approximate number of words. This should be in round figures to the nearest fifty.

Scroll down nine spaces and type, in upper case, the rights you are offering (eg, FIRST BRITISH SERIAL RIGHTS). We'll examine rights in some detail in chapter five.

This completes the cover sheet. An example appears in *Fig 3*.

We now come to the main body of the article. This, and all following pages should be double line spaced. Note that one-and-a-half line spacing is insufficient: there should be a clear line-space between each line of type.

Drop down three lines (always double-spaced) and type, centred, your title in upper case letters.

Drop down one line and type: 'by'.

Drop down one line and type your name or *nom de plume*.

Drop down two line spaces in readiness to commence your article at the left-hand side of the paper. Do not indent the first paragraph.

Leave a good border (about 35mm) around the entire work. This is to accommodate the editor's hand-written alterations and instructions to the printer.

All following paragraphs should be indented five or six spaces,

A Writer,
3 Inkwell Street,
Story Town,
Blottinghamshire,
TT2 6XZ.

Tel: 1111 22222

A POSITIVE REACTION

An article by
Fred Bloggs

1,000 words

FIRST BRITISH SERIAL RIGHTS OFFERED

Fig 3. The cover sheet of an article manuscript.

except those following a heading or a sub-heading. These should be treated like the first paragraph of a work and not be intended at all.

Do *not* leave two double spaces between paragraphs. Many new writers fall into this trap (myself included in days gone by). One double space is usually all that is needed between paragraphs.

An example title page is given in *Fig 4*.

All following pages should contain, at the head of the paper, the title of the work, your name or *nom de plume* and the page number. This heading should be underlined to separate it from the main body of the work. Then drop down at least two spaces before recommencing your typescript. Type to the bottom of the page, irrespective of where a paragraph falls. It is not necessary to use only whole paragraphs on each page. If you finish in the middle of a paragraph on one page, simply carry the remainder over to the following page. To put it another way: keep the same number of lines for each complete page of type.

An example of a following page is given in *Fig 5*.

On the final page, after you have completed the text, drop down a couple of spaces and type a line followed by: 'End.'

At the foot of the page, on the left hand side, type, in single spacing, your real name and address.

Your article manuscript is now complete. Before you send it out check it thoroughly for typing errors. If you have a word processing program which has a spell-checker don't forget to use it. And make sure it is on the correct use of English spelling according to market. English or American.

Short Stories

Short fiction manuscripts should be laid out and typed in the same format as articles, except of course that when it comes to the cover sheet the description of the work will be: 'A Short story by' in place of 'An article by'. Otherwise all details will be the same.

A POSITIVE REACTION

by

Fred Bloggs

When people gather together to socialise they loosen up. Particularly when they take a drink whilst doing so. They spend with less reluctance than they do at other times. They are therefore more susceptible to the impulse buy. Particularly if the price they have to pay is not that much to begin with. If they can be entertained into the bargain they will consider their money well spent. And there is no better example of this than the slot machine.

Today, we live in the age of miniaturisation - particularly where electronics are concerned. And the amusement machine is no exception. Electronic games come in all shapes and sizes, but none so small as the React machine. This is designed to fit almost anywhere and to suit all levels of ability. Whilst its concept is new to Britain it has been established in Europe since 1989, so it is a proven business idea.

For any game to be popular with anyone of no matter what IQ it has to be simple to understand. And that is just the feature the React unit has. Some electronic games are so complicated it almost seems as though you need a degree in mathematics and electronics to be able to participate. This is off-putting to any but the dedicated few. Anyone approaching a React machine won't be put off at the

Fig 4. The title page of an article manuscript.

first hurdle when they read the rules of play. These are few and easy to understand. You simply press a button at a given signal to measure your reaction time.

React is a state of the art electronic package, the result of extensive research. It is a machine for amusement only, the reward for playing being in the improvement of your own previous best score - or as a competition between any number of players to see who can achieve the lowest score.

The machine is compact enough to be sited in prime positions that conventional amusement machines could never exploit, such as a bar top, counter or shelf. Its small size also holds another major benefit: if one location doesn't prove to be particularly lucrative, the unit is small enough to be transported somewhere else simply by unplugging it and carrying it away. This also makes it ideal for short term siting in seasonal locations such as the recreation facilities of camping and caravan parks. All that is needed to set the React to work is a flat surface of less than one square foot plus an adjacent standard 13 amp socket.

Potential earnings from these machines as a business will, of course, vary from one site to another. Those having a constantly changing clientele will prove to be the best: hotels and transit lounges, for example. But if we take a typical monthly revenue at 30 plays per day the figures look something like this: 840 plays per month at 20p = £168 per unit. Subtract 50% for the site owner's split and this gives £81 per unit. Multiplying this by 25 units (a typical size of business) gives

Fig 5. A following page of an article manuscript

Informative Fillers

An informative filler is really a mini-article. As far as the typescript is concerned it should be treated as a cross between a reader's letter and a full-length article. It should be typed but there is no need to include a cover sheet. Begin the main body of your submission, single spaced, with your real name and full postal address in the upper right-hand corner of a sheet of plain A4 paper. Drop down two spaces and type your telephone number and below that drop down three spaces and type the date.

Now move across to the left-hand side of the paper and drop down two spaces before typing the name and address of the publication to which you are making your offer. As with other submissions, address it directly to the editor if at all possible.

Next, drop down four spaces and type what is on offer and add the appropriate number of words. This should be followed, two spaces down, by the rights on offer.

Drop down four spaces and in the centre of the page type, in capital letters, the title of the piece. Everything following the title should be double spaced. Beneath it type 'by', and below that your name or *nom de plume*.

Now for the text itself. Drop down two double spaces and begin at the left-hand margin. As with articles, there should be no indent to the first paragraph nor to any other paragraph which follows a sub-heading. All other paragraphs should be indented five or six spaces. There should be only one double space between paragraphs, as before.

If your filler won't fit a single sheet of paper, ensure the following pages carry, at the top of the page, the title on the left-hand side, your surname in the centre, and the page number in the right-hand corner. All of this should be underlined, just like an article manuscript.

At the end of the piece, drop down three double spaces and type a line followed by the word 'End'. Then drop down to the bottom of the sheet and type your name and address, single spaced, in the left-hand corner.

For an example of a filler manuscript see *Fig 6*.

A. Writer,
3 Inkwell Street,
Story Town,
Blottinghamshire,
TT2 6XZ.

Tel: 1111 22222.

9th May 1996.

A. Scribe,
Editor,
The Toy Town Journal,
1 Article Road,
Magazine Village,
Typesham,
FF6 7BB.

A filler article of 400 words.

First British Serial Rights Offered.

PARAGRAPHS THAT PAY

by

A. Writer

Many people have compelling reasons for wanting to earn money in their spare time.

A high mortgage combined with a low income is one example. But no matter what the

motive for wishing to supplement their income, there are those that simply cannot find

employment to suit their available free moments. Children to look after; elderly or sick

relations to care for; living in a high unemployment area; shift work to contend with -

Fig 6. Page one of a filler manuscript.

Poetry and Verse

A poetry manuscript should have a cover sheet as described for articles, except, of course, that the description of the work should be 'A poem by', followed by your name or *nom de plume*. It is necessary to use a cover sheet because the main body of a poetry manuscript is laid out somewhat differently from those in other areas of writing.

Poems should always be typed in the form they are to appear in the final printed version. If a poem is to appear single spaced then this is how the manuscript should be typed. If the final version is to have odd length indents, this is how they should appear on the typescript. The printer will print whatever he or she sees. It is for this reason that if your poem continues onto a second sheet of typescript without a break, you should type at the foot of the page: 'poem continues, no break'. At the head of the following page you should type: 'poem continues from previous page, no break'.

In all other respects a poetry typescript should be presented as for an article.

Crosswords and Other Puzzles

Puzzle manuscripts do not need to be presented in double spaced type. Other manuscripts are presented in this way to allow the editor to cut and correct and to present them in the house-style associated with his or her publication. These need spaces around them to accept hand-written corrections. Single spacing of puzzles is acceptable because an editor is highly unlikely to comment on such a highly specialised submission. In any event, by its very nature this form of manuscript has plenty of space around it to take the odd comment should it ever prove necessary.

Let's take a look at a crossword manuscript.

A crossword manuscript should comprise of five sheets of white A4 paper: a cover sheet, the clues, the grid, the solutions and a proof of solution.

The cover sheet should be as described for articles except when it comes to the description of the piece. This should make clear what kind of puzzle is on offer: either cryptic or straight.

The second sheet of your submission should contain the clues. Head the page with the word 'CLUES', centred, in upper case. Drop down three or four lines and revert to the left-hand side of the paper. As always, leave a generous margin. Type: 'Across'. Drop down two lines and begin your clues numbered in sequence. After each clue include, in brackets, the number of letters in the solution.

Once you have typed all of your clues across, drop down three or four lines and continue with your clues down, in the same manner.

The third sheet of your submission should simply be a photostat copy of the grid.

The fourth sheet should be a schedule of solutions, laid out in a similar style to the clues (except, of course, the length of solutions will not appear).

The final sheet of the submission is another copy of the grid but this time filled in as a proof that the solutions actually fit. This is best done in a contrasting colour; red is ideal. At the foot of this page on the left type your name and address.

When it comes to other puzzles there are of course many of them and they will look different according to style and degree of complexity, but if you follow the basic guidelines given above no editor should have too much cause for complaint. The watch-word is neatness.

Non-Fiction Books

In principle, non-fiction books should be typed in the same way as articles (double spaced on good quality A4 paper, with generous margins, etc), but with some omissions and some additions.

The rights on offer should not appear anywhere on a book manuscript. The terms and conditions of your offer will form part of a written contract which will be negotiated separately. The same applies to length. The wordage will be agreed as part of the contract and the actual wordage of the completed book can be contained in covering correspondence.

All pages of a book manuscript should carry a heading which includes: the title, the author's surname and the page number. The pages should be numbered consecutively throughout and not chapter by chapter.

Essentially, your manuscript should contain pages similar to those of the final book: it will contain preliminary and end pages. These will be in addition to those of an article manuscript. They have been formulated by convention over the years, although some of these pages are no longer used by all publishers today. But if you include them all, where relevant, the publisher can simply put a line through them if he or she doesn't wish to see them in the finished book.

As the phrase suggests, the preliminary pages are those placed at the beginning of the book before the text begins. They are made up, in order of appearance, like this:

- *Half-title* – the first page carries the title of the book with no additions – not even the name of the author, nor any sub-title that may be used on the cover.
- *Half-title verso* – the reverse of the title page is often left blank, but sometimes, if applicable, this is where other books by the same author, or other titles in the same series, are printed.
- *Title* – this contains the full title of the book, including any sub-title. This page also carries the author's name and the publisher's name.
- *Copyright notice* – this is where the all important copyright notice is placed. (Eventually it will also give the date of first publication, the printing history, the publishers address, and the printer's name and address – but you will not be in a position to know these so you simply leave them out.) Sometimes this is also the page where any dedication is printed should you wish to include one. But note, sometimes

the dedication is included on its own page, following the copyright notice page, with a blank page following that.

● *Contents* – this page gives the table of contents listing the chapter headings, sometimes sub-headings, and associated page numbers. (Of course, you cannot be in a position to know the final printed page numbers at this stage, so you have to leave them blank.) The list of contents can go on for more than one page so the pages that follow will be numbered differently from book to book.

● *List of illustrations* – not always used, but where it is relevant it can also be utilised to include any acknowledgements associated with the illustrations.

● *Foreword* – this is a comment on the book or its author, usually written by a friend or acquaintance of the author, at his or her request. A large body of opinion today says that a foreword does little if anything to enhance the author's reputation or to promote the book and so is better left out.

● *Introduction* – as the name implies the introduction introduces the book to the reader and often outlines what it is all about and why it has been written. Unlike a foreword, a well-balanced introduction can hook the reader by providing an understanding to the book as a whole.

The main body of the book follows, commencing with chapter one. Each chapter should begin on a new page. After the final chapter some end pages are often added, as follows:

● *Appendix* – this is where to include further information on the subject of your book which does not fit neatly into the main text, such as names and addresses of relevant organisations, clubs and associations.

● *Further Reading* – this is where to list other books and periodicals on the subject of your book which may interest its readers and provide them with additional information.

● *Index* – most good non-fiction books include an index, but it cannot be produced at the stage of writing your book.

This can only be produced once page proofs have been printed. (Also, it may not form part of your contract to produce the index.) All you can do at manuscript stage is to include a separate sheet headed 'Index' as a reminder that this has yet to be prepared.

Novels

A novel manuscript is laid out in a similar fashion to a non-fiction book, except that it will have fewer preliminary pages and end pages. There will be no need for a contents page, a list of illustrations, an appendix, or an index.

Illustrations

Open any magazine and you are likely to find an illustration. Even crusty professional journals use them today – perhaps only by way of a photograph of the author, but they are used nonetheless.

Many popular magazines are predominantly illustrative. Indeed, some devote far more space to illustrations than they do to text. Illustrations are a part of everyday reading matter and they are wanted by most editors for at least part of their publications. They are here to stay, so they need to be given some of your attention if you are to succeed as a freelance writer.

Illustrations can make an article more saleable. They also enhance the value of it so that you can expect a higher fee. But pictures must be relevant if they are to make a sale. Whilst articles are often supported by illustrations, short stories are not. Nearly always, short stories are illustrated by the magazine's own hand-drawn artwork.

Novels rarely use pictures whereas non-fiction books often do. Books on interior design, gardening, cartooning or art, could hardly be written without illustrations. Either photographs or drawings. Puzzles too, more often than not need the support of artwork. A crossword could hardly appear in any form without a grid illustration.

The need for artwork, under many circumstances, is a certainty.

Sources of Illustrations

Assuming illustrations are to be used, you have to decide who is to provide them. Are you going to supply them or is the publisher? The simple answer is: it all depends. It all depends on whether we are talking of book-length works or articles as we've said, but it also depends on the target market.

In a book-length work the contract will specify where the responsibility lies. For adult books it will nearly always be the author's job to provide any drawings, photographs, etc, needed as illustrations. However, book contracts are rarely specific about how many illustrations are to be used and what they are to portray. The author is, after all, producing the book, not the publisher. It is therefore for him/her to decide what is to be included.

The author is not *always* expected to provide the illustrations. Sometimes they are provided by a trained artist employed specifically for the task by the publisher. Children's books for example, both fiction and non-fiction, are often profusely illustrated. A high proportion of these illustrations are provided by specialist illustrators rather than the author. Few authors of children's fiction are capable of producing illustrations as well as writing. In these circumstances publishers are well versed in matching artist to author, so leave the task to them. This is even the case with many picture books. The storyline is written by the writer who originated the idea whilst the illustrations come from a professional illustrator.

Occasionally, of course, an illustrator can get together with a writer to produce a book from scratch without any input from a publisher. And this has a certain amount to commend it: the publisher will be saved at least one job, which can make his/her life easier.

There is one occasion when the illustration is *always* provided by the publisher: the cover illustration. Book jacket design is a specialised field. It is effectively part of the book's promotion and as such falls to the publisher to provide it.

When it comes to articles it will often fall to the author to provide any illustrations necessary to accompany them. Sometimes magazines will provide what is necessary, particularly with up-market publications. However, with lower paying outlets it usually falls to the writer to provide anything needed to supplement the words. This is particularly true of very visual work such as craft articles and 'how-to's or anything requiring charts and graphs, such as business articles. It is all a question of market research.

As a rule of thumb, most high circulation glossies will wish to use their own illustrations whereas the lower circulation, lower paying, outlets often prefer their authors to provide them.

Having said that, if there is any doubt about who normally provides illustrations, regardless of level of market and editorial policy, your piece stands a better chance of a sale if it is accompanied by illustrations.

Few magazines today will specify only black and white photographs for their illustrations. Whilst this was so in times gone by, today most printing processes will accept colour prints, even if they are to be used only as the basis for black and white illustrations. And even fewer markets today insist on transparencies for colour (although please be clear that *some* do, so it is wise to check first).

Not all writers are born photographers, of course. Only the operator of a camera can compose the picture and if you are no good at composition, perhaps you had better consider obtaining your illustrations from a professional. If you are inexperienced at illustrating by all means try your hand at it, but leave yourself plenty of time to go out to a professional if your own turn out to be unsaleable.

Those wishing to provide line illustrations could consider the use of a personal computer (PC). Even cheap publishing programs can produce very saleable line diagrams, charts and graphs. If you don't already own a PC it is worth considering buying one, for it can hold many advantages, which we'll look at in a moment.

If you provide the illustrations yourself you will have to find someone to do it for you. An advertisement in one of the photographic magazines is likely to elicit some enthusiastic photographers for you to team up with. Or you could contact someone willing to produce line drawings through one of the many computer magazines.

If you can use ready-made illustrations you could make contact with a picture library. One of the yearbooks could help you here. The *Writers' and Artists' Yearbook* has a classified index of pictures agencies and libraries. This lists many libraries covering subjects from Aerial Photography to Waterways. *The Writer's Handbook* lists almost 300 picture libraries in alphabetical order, giving the specialities of each, often with the sizes of collections available for hire.

Another source of illustrations is product manufacturers. They will usually let you have copyright-free photographs for use with articles that feature them or their products. For them it is free publicity. For you it means a better chance of a sale and the likelihood of a higher fee into the bargain.

If you decide to write with a collaborator perhaps your partner is more of an expert at illustrations than you. A writer/illustrator collaboration can work to good effect, for rarely is a good illustrator a good writer, and vice versa. The drawback here though, is making the financial arrangements. It is doubtful you will find a professional to produce illustrations on spec to go with your on-spec articles. He/she will probably require a flat fee rather than a share of the profits, if any. If, on the other hand, you are writing a book-length work for which you have a contract, it is possible an offer of a share in the royalties could attract a suitable candidate. However, if illustrations form only a small part of the book, a flat fee might be more appropriate.

Types of Illustration

Illustrations can take many forms. In order to decide what you should use you should examine the publications for which you wish to write to see what type they use, if any, and if used to see whether they are black and white or colour. Always determine what your target magazine uses before making a submission. Look to see how many illustrations are used and of what size.

Photographs are a common form of illustration. Taking pictures and having them processed can be very time-consuming, and time is money. So *always* determine the format required by your target magazines before you begin work.

Whilst snapshots are fine for readers' letters, they are of little use when it comes to more up-market work. You'll have to be more professional. Having said that, fully automatic cameras available today make successful photography pretty foolproof. A modern camera in the hands of an amateur is perfectly capable of producing shots which are quite adequate for commercial reproduction.

At one time some photographers carried two cameras: one for colour film and one for black and white. But today this is hardly necessary as with modern processing techniques colour prints can be used to produce a black and white image in a magazine without too much loss of definition.

Photographs should be clear with good contrast and prints should have a glossy finish. Sometimes, transparencies are still demanded by quality magazines for their colour illustrations, particularly cover shots. These should never be mounted in glass but just as they are processed.

Other illustrations come in many forms: diagrams, graphs, sketches, paintings, puzzle grids . . . At one time the artwork for these was often presented on quality Bristol Board. Today, such extravagance is not considered necessary. Good quality 80gsm bond paper will suffice. The same applies to pens. Quality drawings pens are fine, but not altogether essential for simpler illustrations. Felt and fibre-tipped pens are often all that is needed. The acid test is: does it look right? If it does then it is doing the job.

Size of Illustrations

Publishers have differing requirements for illustrations. Film processing and printing techniques are becoming increasingly sophisticated, and we can now process just about anything. For the moment though, we'll look at those that are the most widely accepted today, but be aware that they are by no means the preference of *all* publishers. Again, the watchword is: research.

Illustrations, no matter what type (photographs to cartoons) are nearly always reproduced at a different size in the published version than the original. In most cases they are larger. As a general rule, the aim should be to produce illustrations with a minimum of 50% reduction in mind.

Ideally, photographic prints should be glossy, size 250mm × 200mm (10″ × 8″), although 200mm × 100mm (8″ × 6″ – whole plate) are usually a good enough alternative. Many publications (particularly lower paying ones) will accept 150mm × 100mm (5½″ × 4″). And right at the other end of the scale even passport size photos (50mm × 40mm – 2″ × 1½″) are often used on readers' letters pages.

When it comes to colour slides, 35mm (1½″ × 1½″) is acceptable to most outlets, except when it comes to cover illustrations which should be 60mm × 60mm (2½″ × 2½″).

Paper or Bristol Board illustrations can come in many sizes, but for most uses an A4 sheet (300mm × 210mm – 11½″ × 8¼″) is quite adequate. This is convenient because it fits well with similar sized manuscript pages.

Labelling Illustrations

The text of a book manuscript will refer to each illustration by its unique figure number. Be sure to identify each of your actual illustrations with this same number.

Some book publishers like to see illustrations numbered according to the chapter to which they relate. Figure numbers for chapter two, for example, would begin at 2.1 followed by figure 2.2, and so on. It is simply a question of publisher preference. You need to pick whichever system suits you. If you pick one in opposition to the eventual publisher's preference it is no big deal as it can be altered at editing stage.

Sometimes, photographs can be included in a book but not keyed to the text by figure numbers. Photographs in a biography, for example, may be relevant to the book as a whole but not to any particular passage or chapter. Nevertheless, captions will still normally be required and so these illustrations also need to be keyed to a list of captions with the manuscript.

If you have sufficient space beneath your artwork to write the caption, write it well away from the illustration. Captions are nearly always typeset, so leave sufficient space so yours won't appear in the final illustration. If there is insufficient space for the caption on the face of the illustration, place it on the back. This is best done by way of a self-adhesive label to avoid the damage to the face of the illustration that would occur if you actually wrote on the back. Alternatively, identify photos with a number on the back and supply them together with a schedule of captions keyed to each illustration. These captions should be worded as they are to appear in the final text for the typesetter to copy.

Where to Include Them

If you are to provide illustrations for a book you should include copies with your typescript, but do not identify them with manuscript page numbers. The illustration numbers will suffice. Place all illustrations at the end of their related chapter.

For short works (articles), illustrations should be kept separate from the typescript.

In all instances, package the original illustrations separately from the manuscript. Original illustrations can be delicate and need to be handled with care. It is best to use no form of binding and *never* use paper clips on photographs as they will almost certainly cause damage.

Originals should never be sent with speculative submissions, but should be forwarded only in the event that you secure a sale.

Sidebars

A sidebar is a self-contained supplement to an article which is treated differently to other illustrations because it is typeset rather than reproduced from original artwork. There is no standard set of rules covering what should be contained within one. A sidebar is included to add interest, just like other illustrations. Most often, a sidebar lists the most salient points of an article, or supplements it in some way. The chief points of a business opportunity article for example, could be its start-up costs, staffing levels and projected profits. Sidebars which are a supplement will add information which is not contained within the main body of the text. For example, it could list contact organisations and their addresses.

The most common type of sidebar gives details of where to get more information. A travel article for example, could give the names and addresses of travel agents or specific holiday destinations, such as hotels or caravan parks.

Often, editors will write sidebars themselves, but the astute freelance writer will save him/her the trouble, if such are currently used by a target publication. Submissions containing sidebars can have an edge over competing submissions that do not, much in the same way as manuscripts having other illustrations.

A sidebar in the final text is usually set separately in its own box. But as a submission from an author it should be presented on a separate sheet of paper but in the same manuscript format as the rest of the article. It is an add-on; a tasty morsel on the side. So treat it as such. Make it short and succinct.

Here is a example giving the main points of sidebars:

- A sidebar should be self-contained.

- A sidebar should highlight the main points of an article or give supplementary information about it.
- A sidebar should be set separately in its own box.

The Synopsis

What is a synopsis? *The Penguin English Dictionary* defines it as: 'general view; summary; outline of a plot of a book, play, film etc'. Note that in this definition a synopsis is an outline of a full-length work: 'a book, play, film etc'.

A synopsis should not be confused with an article outline, which is similar to a synopsis but not so detailed and usually in the form of a letter. This isn't to say you cannot have a synopsis of an article. You can. But it is not wise to produce one for such a short work, for if you went to so much trouble you might just as well have written the article and let it speak for itself. It would take about the same amount of effort. A synopsis can only be justified when trying to sell a full-length book. And a non-fiction book at that.

For a first novel, you should usually submit the whole work rather than some sample chapters and a synopsis. Publishers cannot be sure a new novelist could sustain a promising opening right through to the end of a book, and no contract is likely to be offered unless the novel as a whole can be judged. This is not the case with an established novelist, of course, for a track record will offer evidence of competence. And some publishers do prefer to see just a few chapters and an outline from first novelists, so it is best to check.

A first non-fiction book has more chance of consistency than a first novel. If an outline and sample chapters are competently written, it is likely the remainder of the book will follow suit. This being so, first non-fiction books are often commissioned against an idea. That idea, in the main, is usually expressed in written form by way of a synopsis.

Anyone reading a synopsis should be able to gain from it a clear idea of what the proposed book will be all about and roughly how it will be treated. A synopsis forms part of a sales blurb and so it must be presented to the highest possible standard. The object is to make it *sell* an idea so that a contract is offered to develop the idea into a full-length work.

Unlike a manuscript, a synopsis should be typed in single spacing. It should be neat, clean and professional-looking and it should be secured together with a paper clip. Bindings and flashy covers just get in the way and should be avoided.

A synopsis should be as short as possible and still communicate what the book is all about. Many synopses can say what they need to say in four or five pages, whereas others will need more than this in order to cover the ground properly. It is a question of what the book is all about: long book, short book, complex or simple – as well as a host of other factors. A synopsis needs to be explicit but remain succinct.

A book synopsis rarely exists in isolation. It is usually combined with an overall proposal, which we will deal with in the next chapter. A book synopsis should contain:

- A proposed title
- Possible alternative titles
- An outline of the introduction, if any
- Chapter outlines
- An outline of any appendices.

No matter how good a job you make of presenting a synopsis, your idea is unlikely to grab attention if it has an indifferent title. So a title needs some thinking about before a final selection is made. In general, short titles are better than long ones. A title should succinctly summarise the content of the book and it should be easy to remember.

A short title is best because it has to fit along the spine of the book, as well as on the cover. There will however, need to be sufficient words to let the browser know what the book is all about. Sometimes a sub-title helps here. It can be included on the cover but not the spine. But this is all a little premature, for the title of your book is very likely to be changed at some time before it is finally published. You will be ignorant of the new title for most of the time. You are likely to nurture your book through its preliminary stages then right through to the finished manuscript. All this time you will be thinking of it as a king having your chosen title as its crown. Eventually the proofs will arrive – and lo it is headed by the publisher's chosen title and not your own. This you will have to live with for the rest of the book's natural life. So the sooner you get used to the new title the better.

To begin with though, you have no need to worry your head as to the likely final choice. For now, your chosen title has to sell an idea.

If your synopsis does its job and sells the book idea, your proposed title is likely to be used for reference purposes throughout negotiations and, possibly, throughout the time you are writing your book.

As we've said, many publishers are fussy about titles, so make life easy for them and offer a few alternatives to choose from. It may be that none of them is used but they do at least provide food for thought.

If you include an introduction to your book you will need to provide some thoughts on the subject in your synopsis. Often, an introduction is an outline of the book and who it will best serve. You should include something of what this is to say.

The chapter break-downs should appear in the order that you foresee them appearing in the final work. This must be in a logical, ordered sequence to enable the reviewer to envisage exactly what is being proposed. Each outline should be brief and to the point.

If it is your intention to use headings and sub-headings it is a good idea to include them in the synopsis as they will paint a clearer picture than if you use text alone.

State whether or not illustrations are to be included and if so roughly the extent: highly or lightly illustrated. It would be better still if you could be more precise. If you are capable of providing them yourself make this clear. When you first come to an area of the book where you intend to include illustrations, say something like: 'This chapter is to include two illustrations. NB: I would be responsible for providing the illustrations throughout the book.'

The typewriter

As we've said, if you want your commercially-targeted work to have credibility it will have to be typed. You could, of course, employ the services of a typing agency to undertake this work for you from your hand-written draft. But this can be expensive. It is also inflexible. If you have second thoughts and want to rewrite just one word you will have to go back to your typing service to have the alterations made. This is both time-consuming and a waste of hard-earned cash. You would be much better off typing your work for yourself. You don't have to be a master typist to begin with. You may take a while to produce your manuscripts – searching for individual keys, perhaps, when you don't know the layout of the keyboard. But you will soon learn to find them without the need to look. Given time, touch typing of a kind comes to anyone who takes the trouble to try.

Your typewriter doesn't have to be anything special; a second-hand manual machine can be picked up for very little. But if you can afford it, an electronic typewriter has the distinct advantage of producing neat copy irrespective of operator ability. Unlike a manual machine, each key-stroke exerts the same pressure on the ribbon to produce a professional-looking result. Well worth the extra cost.

Unfortunately, typewriters have a major drawback over other equipment that has been made available by advancing technology. Make too many mistakes on a typewriter and a page of text will be beyond correction. You'll have to type the page again. But if you were to invest in some computer equipment you would have no such hassle.

The word processor

What is a word processor? Many new writers ask this. The phrase 'word processor' sounds grand and intimidating. But it needn't be.

To a writer, the word processor is manna from heaven. It can take a great deal of the slog out of writing (or, more importantly, the rewriting). If you want to make changes to your manuscript you don't have to retype it – the word processor does that for you. A word processor is like a typewriter having magical qualities.

When Amstrad introduced their Personal Computer Word Processor (PCW) several years ago it opened up many new possibilities to writers. Effectively, their PCW is a sophisticated substitute for a typewriter which can perform many tasks the typewriter cannot. It is a personal computer that is dedicated to producing typewritten output.

A PCW has a keyboard almost the same as a typewriter but in addition it has a screen on which the typewritten word can be seen, and on which changes can be made without the necessity of retyping. This device can also store text electronically, as well as print it onto paper whenever and as often as you like.

Initially, the PCW was used to produce all manner of typewritten documents from letters to manuscripts. But soon afterwards operating systems that control these wondrous gadgets became more and more sophisticated until all kinds of documents could be produced including those containing graphics. Whilst the PCW is now considered to be dated, it is quite capable of producing acceptable manuscripts provided a good enough printer is used in place of its original, dot matrix, printer. Second-hand PCWs are now relatively cheap.

Today however, all manner of Personal Computer (PC) equipment is available in which word processing is just one of the many functions it can perform.

For the benefit of those who know nothing of PCs and how they are put together, let's take a look at a typical example. The equipment needed to produce the written word is hardware and software. Let's consider these two elements separately.

Hardware
The pieces of equipment which form a PC are as follows:

1. A computer
2. A keyboard
3. A monitor
4. A printer.

All of these items can be purchased separately, although very often they are marketed together. Sometimes, sound is an option offered for which speakers would be required – but this of course is not necessary for use with word processing software.

The computer itself is the piece of equipment which receives and processes your instructions to provide you with the end product you wish to print. How this unit performs this task is academic and you do not need to understand any of its intricacies to be able to use it. But you do need to be aware that computers have different capacities. Some have a much greater capability to store information than others and can handle output at greater speeds. As far as the writer is concerned, a computer doesn't need to be too grand, although the further up the scale you go the faster you will be able to work and the more software facilities will be open to you.

The keyboard is much like that of any typewriter, but there are some additional keys which are provided to give instructions to the computer. If you can use a typewriter you will have no trouble adapting. And if you can't, it won't take you long to learn.

The monitor is just like a television screen. Your work is displayed on it as you progress. Monitors can display in black type on white background (although other colour backgrounds are also common) or in full colour. If you use a computer purely as a word processor, you won't need a colour version.

Types of printer can vary. The daisy wheel printer is hardly seen these days and won't be offered with new equipment: the remaining printers usually available will be. These are: dot matrix, ink jet, and laser.

The quality of the final copy from these printers varies. Dot matrix printers are the cheapest option and their quality of image reflects this fact, although in themselves the quality varies, too. The typeface on this sort of printer is produced by a number of pins forming the shape of a letter and reproducing it on the paper by striking a ribbon, much like a conventional typewriter. Whilst these have improved in recent years, they are seldom considered good enough for manuscript presentation these days. They are also noisy.

At the other end of the scale is the laser printer. This is fast and produces quality results. But these are expensive and not necessary to produce the quality of print required for manuscript presentation.

The ideal printer these days is the ink jet. It is fast, quiet and provides very good results at an affordable price.

Software

No matter what computer hardware you have it will be no good to you without some software to run it. Some software packages are often provided free with a set of hardware as an incentive to buy. Fortunately for the writer, you will often be given a word processing package as part of the deal. If you are, you will have all you need to get started.

If your package doesn't include word processing software and you need to buy some, you should examine a few copies of some current dedicated PC magazines to see what is in vogue. Installing any new software into a computer is becoming easier all the time and by the time you read this book it will be easier still. The user handbook will tell you how to go about it.

The facilities offered by different word processing programs vary, but these days all programs should cover just about anything you need. The main thing to look for is the ability of the computer screen to display precisely what it will print out in hard copy. This is known as WYSIWYG – which means: 'what you see is what you get'. This is a feature any discerning writer will wish to use.

Just about all programs will now allow you to alter your words on screen to your heart's content. You can switch text around from one page to another; alter the page layout; change the margin width; revise from single to double spacing (as well as any other line spacing you choose); use automatic headings; automatic page numbering; file and save; and print one page of text, several pages, or all of it at your command. You can also check your grammar, check your spelling (English or American), or keep a running word count. All of these features are today standard with most word processing software packages.

A word processor is by no means an essential tool but if you choose to use one it can speed up your writing, eliminate mistakes and generally make life easier. And programmes are becoming easier to use all the time. A computer is a worthwhile investment for anyone who wants to take their writing seriously.

5

Marketing

Agents

Do you need an agent? And if you do, at what stage of your writing career should you go about finding one?

These are questions which have different answers for different people. It all depends on the area a writer is to cover and his/her own natural marketing ability. Many writers believe an agent will give them a better chance of becoming published. And they are probably correct. But no agent can help you if you cannot write. And you are unlikely to find an agent to represent you if you cover only limited ground. If you write the occasional short story, article or reader's letter then you certainly won't get one to act for you. There just wouldn't be sufficient mileage in it. It is simply a question of economics. A 10% cut of the revenue from a few articles or stories wouldn't pay the agent's postage costs let alone provide a worthwhile income. Unless you are particularly well-known it is unlikely an agent would take you on for anything other than book-length works. This means that alongside marketing your own short works such as articles and short stories, the agent will market your books as a separate exercise.

There are 'fors' and 'againsts' for having an agent. Personally, I use one. This book was placed by my agent. He markets my full-length projects whilst I continue to sell my own short works. I find this arrangement suits me. Trying to sell book-length projects would take up too much of my precious writing time if I undertook it myself. On the other hand, regular contact with magazine editors is good for the sales of my short works; it helps me to sell most of what I write.

I was lucky in finding an agent. It happened almost by accident. It was at the time when I was endeavouring to sell my first book. I'd sent my proposal to sixteen different publishing houses without success. Many of them had made encouraging noises about its saleability, but all said it wasn't quite right for them. Then the sixteenth suggested I try a particular agent. I contacted him and he took me on. He sold that book within four weeks. In my experience, the answer to the question: 'Do agents help to sell books?' is positively: 'Yes'. They know the market and have the contacts to be able to exploit it. Whilst an author can undertake his/her own market research, he/she cannot possibly hope to compete with the knowledge of an established agent who is in touch with publishers all the time.

No agent will take you on unless he/she believes your work is saleable, of course. That's what agents are for. That is how they make a living. If they don't sell work they starve. So you have to have at least a *basically* saleable product. First novels are notoriously difficult to sell. So yours would have to be exceptional to attract an agent.

Some authors are just too emotional to market their own full-length work. Rejection is too painful for them. An agent offers such people a buffer. They will be blissfully ignorant of all the rejections an agent receives on their behalf, so they won't anguish over them.

One of the major advantages of having an agent is that publishers like to do business with them. Publishers know that an agent, at least, must be happy a book is saleable to promote it in the first place. An agent saves them the initial problem of a first sift.

Whilst an agent can be your sales front, you still have to put a sensible sales package together for him/her to handle. He/she will try to sell your proposal or completed manuscript in the same way that you would have to attempt it. Sometimes an agent may recommend some revisions to improve the chances of a sale. You would be wise to listen. Commissions are an agent's livelihood; they wouldn't waste time recommending changes if they didn't think they would improve the book's chances. But remember, agents are not there to provide criticism or advice to beginning writers. They will only comment on promising proposals.

What Can an Agent Do?

The main function of an agent is to sell work – to as many outlets as possible. It is an agent's job to assess a manuscript's potential and to identify any publisher that is likely to be interested in it. The books produced by most publishers follow a trend. Once the agent has identified that trend he/she can know with some degree of certainty whether or not that publisher is likely to be interested in a particular book. A good agent will know what is in vogue – what is selling and what is old hat. An agent also knows how to go against the trend. If an agent has a manuscript that has merit and yet must compete in a market of many others, he/she will need to know how to angle an approach to a publisher in order to make a sale against the odds.

An agent gets to know the detailed workings of the major publishing houses and the kinds of books they are searching for or are likely to be interested in. And remember, a publisher automatically knows a book has some merit if an agent is prepared to handle it. An agent gives you an edge.

Nevertheless, agents, like publishers, sometimes let a bestseller slip through their fingers. They do not have a one hundred percent foolproof method of picking all the winners. So you need to sell the idea of your book to an agent first.

But if you can sell your book to an agent, why not sell it direct to a publisher and cut out the middle-man? Well, an agent knows the wrinkles. He/she will know what is a good offer and what is indifferent. An agent should be able to build on an indifferent offer to make it into a good one. If you are new to the publishing scene you simply won't have the experience of the marketplace. An agent will know these things and advise you accordingly.

Apart from having a limited knowledge of the marketplace, authors are notoriously bad negotiators – mainly because it is not usually in an author's character to haggle. It embarrasses them to talk money. An agent is a useful intermediary in this and in any other area of negotiation. If there is anything you do not wish to discuss with your publisher you can pass it through your agent. An agent will know what is current practice and will angle the talk accordingly. It is his/her job to win the best possible deal. It is also part of an agent's job to vet the contract to ensure your rights are protected as much as possible. Certainly to ensure there is nothing definitely contrary to your interests.

An agent may have a say in translation and book club rights, large print rights, electronic rights, film rights, radio and TV rights. An agent will also be versed in selling export and foreign language rights. Where a potential supplementary market for a book exists, and does not form part of a book contract, an agent can endeavour to sell those rights elsewhere. This is something most authors would never consider doing for themselves.

An agent will look after your financial interest in other ways too, such as chasing up a publisher when a statement is due and hence extract your royalties on time.

But if you are a new author you must be realistic about your expectations. Don't ask too much of an agent to begin with. Agents aren't charities. They might be able to get you only a small advance on royalties and the book may end up making just a small amount of money, but at least you will have seen yourself in print – perhaps something you may not have been able to achieve alone.

How Much Do Agents Charge?
An agent will only take on a writer if he/she believes that in the long term there is a good chance of him/her making a reasonable

amount of money from writing. You have to remember that very few authors actually make enough at writing to live on and so in turn few will be able to provide sufficient commission for an agent to live on, even when that is combined with the revenue from others of similar limited earning potential.

Agents are a little like authors, in a way, for initially they undertake all of their work on-spec and get paid only if they make a sale. They therefore have to be sure the authors they choose to represent can come up winners. An agent lives on a royalty, the minimum of which, these days, is likely to be 10%. The author of a first book is likely to take a year over producing it at an advance of no more than £1,000. 10% of £1,000 is just £100. An agent would have to have a great many clients at this level to make any kind of living at all. Therefore, he/she is looking for something more than a one-book-author. This is why a great many agents will only take on established authors. They are not in the business of teaching authors how to write, but rather how to market saleable work.

Until recent times the standard commission rate for an agent was 10% of all income derived from sales generated by him/her in the UK. Today however, many agents demand more than this. Twelve and a half per cent seems to be becoming as common as 10% these days, although some agents charge anything up to 20% on all home sales.

It is common practice for charges on earnings from foreign sales to be higher than home sales. This is because an agent's expenses are higher. It involves not just additional postage and telephone costs, but often an agent in the country where he/she is seeking to sell work. In other words he/she acts as an agent's agent.

An agent's fees on short works such as articles and short stories are always likely to be higher than for book-length works, as the associated overheads work out so much more, word for word, than for full-length works.

It is unusual in the UK, even today, for agents to charge a

reading fee. Indeed, any agent who is a member of The Association of Authors' Agents will have agreed not to charge such a fee. If you come across an agent who demands up-front money before looking at what you have to offer, you would be well advised to seek alternative representation.

When you sign a book contract through an agent, all monies paid against that contract will be paid to your agent rather than to you. The agent will then take his/her percentage commission before passing payment onto you. There is no problem with this as you would have to pay the appropriate commission anyway. But it does have one major advantage: if the agent doesn't receive the advance or royalties on time he/she will chase them up. This saves you a delicate job.

Royalty statements are notorious for their lack of coherence. Usually, they consist of scrambled rows of figures which are difficult, if not impossible, for the average author to comprehend. An experienced agent will have more chance than you have of seeing what it all means. If he/she doesn't understand it, it will fall to him/her to obtain clarification from the publisher.

The beauty of having an agent is that you only pay for the service if he/she performs. All their costs on telephone calls and postage whilst trying to sell your work, costs *you* nothing until you are successful. Then it will cost you only a percentage of what you earn. In what other line of work do you have the luxury of paying for a service only if it succeeds?

Agent's Contracts

Often there is no formal agreement between author and agent – except, perhaps, for covering letters from the agent accepting the author and the author's acceptance of the rate of commission. Occasionally though, agents do come up with a contract for an author to sign. Clearly, in this event the contract needs careful examination to see what rights you would be signing away and which ones remain (or are to be enhanced) to your benefit.

If you do engage the services of a literary agent, ensure the agreement between you is clear. Unless you specify that these services are for just one book it could be that he/she will look for a percentage of *all* your earnings from writing. Sometimes a contract will specify a royalty payment on the earnings from all an author's future output. This is fine so long as the agent does process all of it, but, as we've said, usually an author will continue to market his/her own short works. In this event a deduction of royalties on these by the agent can hardly be justified. The same can be said for future books. If it is your intention that an agent simply acts for one book, ensure this is spelled out in the agreement.

If you want to be sure that any appointment letter is fair you could insist on the use of the standard appointment letter recommended by The Association of Authors' Agents. For details of how to obtain a copy write to:

The Association of Authors' Agents,
5th Floor,
The Chambers,
Chelsea Harbour,
London,
SW10 0XF.

Sometimes an agent will propose a more formal arrangement of a contract than a simple exchange of letters. If you are offered a detailed contract, you should seek professional advice before signing it. If you are a member of The Society of Authors you can seek their advice; alternatively you should seek the guidance of a lawyer.

You can terminate your agreement with an agent at any time, of course, but remember he/she will continue to receive commission on any revenue on work which has already been negotiated on your behalf during the life of the agreement.

It should be noted that no matter what form of contract you enter into with your agent, an agent does not enter into a contract with a publisher. The contract is between the publisher and the author; the agent merely acts as a go-between.

Where to Find an Agent

The easiest way to find an agent is to examine *The Writer's Handbook* and the *Writers' and Artists' Yearbook*. The *Handbook* carries 150 UK agents and a similar number of American agents. Each entry describes the type of work handled and the level of commission charged. The *Yearbook* covers a similar number of entries from the UK and the USA. It also covers entries from other countries. It lists the areas of work handled together with associated charges.

Before consulting either of the yearbooks it is wise to ensure it is up-to-date. In common with periodicals, agents and their details change from time to time so it is wise to research a current source of information.

How to Choose an Agent

To choose an agent you need to undertake some market research, much in the same way that you would for marketing your work with magazines. Some agents handle only fiction, some only non-fiction. Some handle TV and radio whereas others do not. Agents, like publishers, normally specialise, so choose your prospective agent with care. It is pointless querying an agent who doesn't handle your kind of material.

Agencies come in all sizes from one person to a large organisation. But an organisation's size doesn't necessarily tell you a great deal about its capabilities. Just because an agency is big doesn't necessarily mean it will always be good. And just because an agency is a one-person-band doesn't have to mean it is bad. As with all spheres in life, it is about people. If you pick the right person to suit you and your wares then you are likely to sell books. The trick is finding an agency that is good for you.

Those new to the writing scene may feel more comfortable with a smaller agency (a one off) because they feel they get more personal attention. And for the newcomer to writing this will almost certainly be the case. But it still needs to be the right one for you.

A good agent will only handle what he/she considers to be saleable. He/she has to retain credibility with publishers. If he/she sends them just any old thing the publisher will soon begin to treat that particular agent with the same caution as any un-solicited contribution received direct from an author. A good agent is respected by publishers, for they know he/she will have weeded out all the non-starters. It is therefore obvious that publishers will look at work from reputable agents first, in preference to those unsolicited submissions from authors and offerings from undiscriminating agents.

If an agent takes you on, he/she should do all he/she can to represent you. He/she should try to sell your work to the best possible advantage. The trick is finding one that will do so. Look to see if they are members of The Association of Authors' Agents. This is always a good starting point, for members of the Association are bound by a code of practice produced by the Association. However, this is not the only test for some of the biggest literary agencies aren't members of the Association. The safest way to find a good agent therefore is by recommendation.

As we have said, if you are ambitious you will need to choose your agent with care; you may have to work with him/her for a long time to come. And once you have chosen your target you need to aim at it in such a way that it will be difficult for it to refuse you.

In common with editors, agents have likes and dislikes. That isn't to say that what they like is necessarily good or what they dislike is bad. But it is their line of country and it is up to you to ensure that it suits you. So look up one of the yearbooks to see what category of books are handled by the various agencies.

Approaching an agent is just as difficult as approaching a publisher. You are stuck in the inevitable Catch 22 – publishers only want to read scripts from agents and agents only want to accept published writers. So your approach needs to be enthusiastic. If you are ambitious this will help your cause. Agents will be more interested in you if you are likely to be able to produce more than one book. You need to come across as someone with a future. To do this you'll need to put together an approach letter complete with a copy of your *curriculum vitae*. We'll come to this later in the chapter.

Do-It-Yourself

George Bernard Shaw once said, 'Literature is like any other trade; you will never sell anything unless you go to the right shop.' No professional writer would argue with that. No writer, no matter how good, can afford to do without detailed market research, irrespective of what area of writing is being considered. Articles, short stories, novels, non-fiction books – all need to be market-researched prior to an offer being made. This is even true of markets you've once been familiar with but have not seen for a while. Editorial policies change, as do the people that make them, so the look of any outlet can change dramatically – sometimes overnight.

You need to target a publisher then read several of its products to be sure your aim is straight. The approach to this can vary a little though, depending on whether you are considering selling a short piece or a book-length work.

Short Works
When trying to find a target outlet for a short piece of work you need to examine several different publications to see what type of readership they are trying to attract. The articles contained in *Woman's Weekly* would not necessarily appeal to the readers who buy *Vogue*. The readership for each of these magazines is likely to be quite different. This is because the subjects covered by them, and their treatment, are quite different. More obviously, it would be pointless to submit a short story to a magazine that uses only features.

The same principle applies to themes. You need to write about topics usually covered by a particular outlet. If certain areas of discussion have never been covered by a publication it is probably because the magazine doesn't want to use them. So don't fall into the trap of sending something totally out of the ordinary for that particular publication. Instead, examine its features to see what areas are covered and in what style. Take a look at all of the editorials (and the advertisements) to see what age range they are targeted at. Also are they aimed at male or female readers – or perhaps both? The magazine for single readers or a family audience? What about the average reader's income? Do these readers have money to spare or does the magazine feature cost-saving articles?

Examine the overall length of articles and the writing style. Does the magazine use short paragraphs and simple sentences? Or is its style more sophisticated? Does it use straightforward text or break it up with headings and sub-headings?

What subjects does the magazine cover? Is it a general interest magazine or is it specialised? An angling article may just scrape into a general interest magazine but I wouldn't try to sell it to a tennis journal.

Are articles illustrated? If so, by what method? Black and white or colour? Photographs or line drawings? Are cartoons ever used to embellish the text?

Now to more fundamental market research. Have a look to see how much of the magazine looks like it is written by staff writers and how much of it is bought in. Look at the names of the contributors. If they don't appear on the credits page, there is a good chance they are by a freelance. Regular features are usually by staff writers whereas one-offs are often bought in. Don't waste your energies trying to muscle in on staff-written features. You won't win.

Also, have a look at the editorial notes on the credits page. Many magazines welcome freelance submissions and say so – whereas others do not and make this fact quite clear in their small print.

Books

Much of what we have said about short works also applies to books. Subject, treatment, length and readership all need to be considered when seeking an outlet for a manuscript. Perhaps though, you need to be yet more of a salesperson. The odds against having a book accepted are even greater than for short work. More than half a million book manuscripts are offered for sale each year, of which less than 90,000 are ever published. This doesn't present the unpublished author with very good odds. So it is important to give your book the best possible chance it can have. In such a competitive environment you must give it an edge over the field by taking George Bernard Shaw's advice and going to the right shop. Clearly, to become a successful writer you must be prepared to learn how to sell. No book, no matter how brilliantly written, no matter how well constructed, will ever find its way onto the bookshelves in the shops unless it is properly marketed. Do not send a novel to a publishing house which publishes no fiction and do not submit a non-fiction book to a house publishing only novels. You'll get nowhere. Don't antagonise publishers by lack of research – your name is likely to become known and you won't be looked at again.

Book publishers vary in what they are prepared to publish. Each has a policy which, usually, it sticks to. One publisher may specialise in scientific works whereas another will handle nothing but romantic novels. No matter how compelling your spy chiller may be, the scientific publisher will not touch it.

Make a list of possible publishers. Then research them. You may already own some books by them. If you are interested in their subjects this is likely to be the case. Study them, then go in search of others at your local library. Ensure your proposed book fits in with the kind of thing they publish. If it doesn't, have a look at another possible outlet and repeat the process until you find one that fits the bill precisely. Then go for it.

A helping hand

To assist you with your market research you should consider obtaining at least one of the following reference works. Whilst they should not be considered to be a substitute for an actual examination of your target outlets they can nonetheless cut out a good deal of time in helping you to make some initial selections.

Writers' and Artists' Yearbook. Published by A & C Black (Publishers) Ltd, annually. More than 600 British and 200 overseas magazines and newspapers are covered by the Yearbook, giving editorial requirements and rates of pay. Whilst this is only a fraction of the markets available (about 7–8% of them) it is nonetheless a good starting point for those who have only a limited knowledge of the literary marketplace. The Yearbook also lists more than 700 British and 350 overseas book publishers and the literary areas they cover. It also lists outlets for poetry, music, plays and broadcasting. Other lists cover literary agents, art, picture libraries, literary prizes, societies and editorial services. There are also some excellent articles covering: magazines, poetry, International Standard Book Numbering, vanity publishing, theatre, television, radio, agents, art, music, prizes, clubs, research, copyright, tax, libel, social security, publishing agreements, public lending rights, manuscript preparation, word processing, proof correction and translations. This volume can be ordered through any book shop or it can be obtained direct from the publisher:

A & C Black (Publishers) Ltd,
35 Bedford Row,
London,
WC1R 4JH.

The Writer's Handbook. Published by The Macmillan Press Ltd, annually. This gives the editorial requirements of around 150 newspapers and 500 magazines, as well as the areas covered by some 750 UK and Irish book publishers. It also lists literary agents, broadcasters, theatres, associations, research services, editorial services, literary prizes and awards, writers' courses, press cutting agencies, libraries, prizes and grants. On top of this there are articles on the subject of selling, poetry, workshops, broadcasting, copyright, libel, income tax and VAT. The Handbook can be ordered through any book shop or it can be obtained direct from the publisher:

The Macmillan Press Ltd,
4 Little Essex Street,
London,
WC2R 3LF.

The Magazine Writer's Handbook. Published every two years by Allison and Busby. This gives in-depth editorial requirements of 70 popular magazines, which are said to be looking for freelance material. Each entry gives: the target readership and editorial policy, the subjects dealt with, the regular columns and features, the type and length of articles and short stories used, the number of 'writer-initiated' articles and short stories accepted per year, how best to approach the editor, how long you may have to wait for a decision, some idea of the likely payment. This publication also takes a look at free London magazines, daily newspapers, 'literary' magazines, and small press magazines. There are also articles on making submissions, writing picture-story scripts, writing letters to the editor, associations for writers, competitions, useful addresses, the writer's bookshelf, and word processing for writers. This volume can be ordered from any book shop or it can be obtained direct from the publisher:

Allison and Busby,
179 Kings Cross Road,
London,
WC1X 9BZ.

The Book Writer's Handbook. Published every two years by Allison and Busby. This is a similar concept to *The Magazine Writer's Handbook* and covers much of the same ground but outlines the requirements of some 100 book publishers. It contains useful information on editorial policy, category of books published, likely payment rates, preferred ways of submitting ideas or manuscripts and how long you will probably have to wait for a decision. There are also articles about presentation, word processing, trade unions, self-publishing, Public Lending Right, and conferences. This volume can be ordered from any book shop or direct from the publisher at the address given above.

Willings Press Guide. Published annually in two volumes (one UK and one overseas) by Reed Information Services. This guide rightly describes itself as: 'a comprehensive, accurate and informative guide to the press'. The term 'press' includes: 'newspapers, free sheets, magazines, journals, newsletters and other publications appearing on a regular basis. In practical terms this means anything published regularly at least once a year.' Each publication listed gives full communication details of publishing, editorial and advertising offices. Also shown, where available, is the year established, price, frequency, circulation, key personnel, editorial content, agency commission, advertising rates and mechanical data and readership/target audience. Whilst the 'summary of content' section is extremely brief, the guide can point you in the direction of many more commercial magazines than the other guides. It carries 2,500 pages of information on current publications, of which 1,400 pages cover the UK alone. The UK volume lists over 13,500 magazines, journals and newspapers. A great many of the publications listed will not be found on news-stands and so won't be the target of many a freelance pen. Those who *can* be bothered to seek out these lesser known publications are bound to have more chance of having their work accepted than those who stick to mainstream magazines. Whilst this guide would be considered by most new writers to be far too expensive to be purchased for personal use, a copy will almost certainly be located in your local reference library. Those wishing to obtain their own copy can order one through any book shop, or direct from:

Reed Information Services,
Windsor Court,
East Grinstead House,
East Grinstead,
West Sussex,
RH19 1XA.

Writer's Market. Published annually in America by Writer's Digest Books. Writers worldwide have been using this market guide since it was first published in 1921. It carries over 1,000 pages of helpful articles and interviews with top professionals, as well as its main thrust of market outlets. It covers 4,000 listings of buyers of freelance work, including their names, addresses, submission requirements and contact person. It is available in Britain from:

Freelance Press Services,
Cumberland House,
Lissadel Street,
Salford,
Manchester,
M6 6GG.

The International Directory of Little Magazines and Small Presses. An American volume, published annually by Dustbooks. This publication carries well over 900 pages of nothing but listings of small press magazines from around the world together with their editorial requirements, both fiction and non-fiction. Amongst these are many British listings. It is an ideal reference work for any writer in the early stages of a writing career when financial gain is not of prime importance. A descriptive leaflet on this directory, giving the current price, is available in exchange for an International Reply Coupon, which can be obtained from any Post Office. The address is:

Dustbooks,
PO Box 100,
Paradise,
California 95969,
USA

Freelance Market News. This is an A4 newsletter, published eleven times a year by Freelance Press Services. This is an invaluable aid to all freelance writers of all levels of writing ability. It is devoted to providing up-to-date markets, both in Britain and overseas. It covers a broad spectrum of publications from small press to national glossies and gives their editorial requirements, and often rates of pay, for both fiction and non-fiction. The newsletter is available on subscription only from Freelance Press Services, at the address given above.

Rights

When you come to sell your work you will need to decide what rights to offer. Essentially, these will vary according to the length of work to be sold.

Short Works
When you offer a short story or an article to a magazine for publication for the first time you will usually offer First British Serial Rights. This means that you are offering a work of your own, which has not been published before, to a serialised publication. This gives the publisher the right to publish your work for the first time and once only in Britain. If it wishes to use

it again at some future date it must pay you for it again (at a rate to be agreed). You retain the right to sell the work anywhere else in the world, for the first time. Once published in this country, you may offer the work again to another publisher under the terms Second British Serial Rights. (Then Third, then Fourth, and so on.) These subsequent rights are seldom bought however, and so they usually command a much lower fee than First Rights.

Once you have sold your work for the first time you could then think of syndicating it via a professional, rather than attempting to resell it yourself. Syndication is the selling and reselling of work, usually previously published work, via an agency. If you already have an agent he/she may be able to undertake this task for you, but, more usually, there are syndicates that specialise in this area of marketing. An outline of syndicates and what each has to offer can be found in the *Writers' and Artists' Yearbook*.

It is rare for a publisher to ask you to sell it the copyright in a work. If it does, think hard — all future profit from the work will belong to the publisher and not to you. If it wishes to buy the copyright you should expect to be paid a much higher fee than you would for the First British Serial Rights.

Full-Length Works

When it comes to selling the rights to a book things are not quite so straightforward. The question of rights in a book will be covered by the publisher's agreement. Publishing contracts vary from one to another, as well as from one author to another, so all agreements should be read very carefully to ensure you get the best deal that you can. If you have an agent he/she can vet the contract for you, but if you are to go it alone this burden rests squarely with yourself. You need to read each clause carefully to see that you are getting what you deserve. If you are a member of one of the writer's societies, either The Society of Authors or The Writers' Guild of Great Britain, you can ask it to vet the contract you are offered and to supply you with written advice on its acceptability.

If you are dealing with a publisher who has agreed a Minimum Terms Agreement with these organisations you could be offered such a contract, in which case you should not have too much cause for complaint. We'll take a look at the Minimum Terms Agreement in the next chapter.

You should be even more cautious of selling the copyright in a book than you should for short works. A bestselling book can earn far more pro-rata than any short piece. In some cases, where you are to write only a small section of a work, such as an entry in an encyclopaedia for example, it may make sense to part with your copyright. If you don't, the payment of royalties becomes far too unwieldy. In just about all other instances though, you are usually better off retaining copyright.

One of the problems with selling copyright is that you have no certain way of knowing what the sales potential for the work is likely to be. It could sell in a big way or it may not sell at all. If it sells big you could end up the loser, for you probably would have earned more from the work had you insisted on a royalty. On the other hand, if the work flops you could end up the winner of the deal. The choice is yours, although the majority of professional writers always stick out for a royalty – just in case they hit the big time.

Submitting work

Once you have undertaken market research you need to put together your ideas and make an offer to your chosen outlet. There are two ways of doing this. You can either offer a complete work or you can sell an *idea* before you begin to write.

Offering Complete Works
Most short works are best submitted complete 'on-spec'. You would spend so much time describing a 1,000 word article in a query letter that you might just as well write the piece and let it speak for itself. And it is pointless to try to sell a short story by

outline – you would never succeed. There is no way an editor could know how a story outline is likely to write up. The same idea expressed by two different authors is unlikely to bear any similarity. One could be attention-grabbing from start to finish, whilst the other could be a complete bore. On the other hand, you can tell a great deal of how an article is likely to look once it is written up.

The unsolicited article manuscripts which arrive with monotonous regularity in all publishers' offices are known in the trade as the 'slush pile'. In many instances these submissions don't get nearly the same attention that invited works receive and usually justly so, for a great many aspiring writers simply do not know how to go about submitting work in an acceptable form. Needless to say, only a small proportion of the slush pile ever gets published. So, you need to ensure yours stands out from the crowd in the way it is presented. Make it so clean and neat an editor will *want* to read it.

Many freelance writers believe complete works should never be offered under cover of a letter; they maintain work should stand on its own merits. But I would challenge such a stance. I believe a link between writer and editor, no matter how tenuous, has to be better than nothing at all.

Your cover letter should be brief and to the point (i.e. don't waste an editor's time with waffle). A couple of sentences are all it takes:

Here for your consideration is a 1,000 word article entitled *How to Service Your Own Gearbox*. I hope you like it.

It is worthwhile addressing your letter to the editor by name to give it that personal touch. If the blurb in your chosen magazine doesn't give the editor's name (although most of them do), ring the magazine's switchboard to ask for it.

If you have some qualification for writing the piece, you should say so. This will give your offering more authority:

Here for your consideration is a 1,000 word article entitled *How to Service Your Own Gearbox*. I have written the piece around my fifteen years' experience as a motor mechanic. I hope you like it.

Selling an Idea

When it comes to a longer, more involved article it may be wise to interest an editor in the idea before writing it up. It is pointless to expend a great deal of time and effort in research and writing if the idea behind a proposed work is in itself not saleable. You therefore need to write to your target editor saying why you believe your piece would be of interest. Say why you are qualified to write it. This may be because of your work, like the motor mechanic and the gearbox, or it might be because of your extensive research. Either way you need to detail why your idea will suit a particular outlet. Effectively, this will be a brief (very brief) synopsis of your ideas, but contained within the body of your letter.

Also outline any past publishing successes you may have had, even if these aren't related to the subject-matter of the idea in question. Some editors like to see hard evidence of your track record before they are prepared to commission a piece. This can be done by providing some cuttings of your previously published work, on a similar theme, perhaps, to the idea you are currently trying to sell. But don't overwhelm an editor with examples. Always remember that time is precious, and reading takes time.

These details will be sufficient for an editor to decide whether or not your idea deserves further investigation. If it does, it is unlikely that you will be commissioned to write the piece, particularly if you have never written for the magazine before, but you will probably be asked to write it up and submit it on spec. Whilst this is not ideal, it is a great deal better than writing up the entire piece in the *hope* that it may be of interest. At least now it is unlikely to be dismissed out of hand. You can refer to the editor's stated interest when you submit your piece, which will do a great deal to rekindle interest. And even if your piece is returned it is unlikely to be in the form of an outright rejection but a request for some changes to be made. You will then truly be on the road to a final sale.

When it comes to marketing a full-length non-fiction work, you will need more than just a cover letter to sell your idea. You should also submit a proposal and a sample chapter or two.

Lay out your letter in exactly the same way that you would lay out any other letter, but be sure to give your telephone number. Editors are busy people who are nearly always under pressure. They may therefore want to talk to you urgently to clear some point which has to fit in with their publishing programme.

The main body of the letter should be straightforward. Suppose you had to compose a covering letter offering the book you are reading right now. What would you include in it? As always, it would need to be brief. It would need to outline what was being offered using the minimum of words. Try this:

Would you be interested in publishing a book which sets out to answer the many questions posed by would-be writers who aspire to see their work in print? I believe such a volume would sell exceptionally well, for the potential audience is vast. My ideas on such a work are included in the enclosed proposal.

I look forward to your views.

When it comes to preparing your proposal, you need to type it up, single spaced, as one document. You need to include in it some or all of the following:

- An outline and market need
- Target audience
- Approximate length
- Author qualifications
- Synopsis.

Go to your local library and pick up some non-fiction books at random. Read the blurb on the back cover, or fly-leaf, of each one. You will note that almost without exception each will outline what the book is all about and who it is intended to reach. And it will do this in just a few paragraphs. Your outline needs to follow a similar pattern.

Not only will a good outline help to sell your book it is also likely you will be able to rewrite it to make an excellent introduction to the final book.

Here is the outline I used to sell this volume:

This book would answer the many questions posed by enthusiastic amateur writers aiming to break into print. All too often, emerging freelance writers become hooked on words without having had the benefit of some formal training. Surprisingly, the unknowns confronting these aspiring scribes are more often about the writing process than they are about creativity.

When I was editor of *Mosaic*, a small press magazine for writers, my mail often contained questions from subscribers that were of a technical rather than a creative nature. It struck me that a book covering such topics would be of interest and help to emerging writers. In an endeavour to confirm this view I approached one hundred writers' circles and asked them to let me have a note of the questions most posed by their groups. I included with my enquiry a schedule of ninety-one topics designed to jog memories. These covered all aspects of writing, both creative and otherwise. In all, I posed over one hundred and fifty questions covering both short and book-length topics, fiction and non-fiction. In the majority these queries related to topics other than the creative face of writing. By far the highest proportion covered marketing in one form or another. Others included English usage, copyright, presentation, publishing, as well as a host of other related headings. Overall, the results of the survey showed a common need for answers to questions on the writing process. This book sets out to fulfil that need.

A publisher has to be persuaded that there is a market for the ideas behind your book. You need to identify this market, including its size. It certainly needs to be large enough to be able to sell a minimum print run of 2,000 copies to make the venture viable. The larger the sales potential, the easier it will be to persuade the publisher to offer you a contract to write the book. It may take several hundred words to outline this need or it may take just a couple of sentences. It all depends on how easy it is to identify and how many groups of people it is likely to reach. The target audience for this book was identified in just five sentences:

> The potential readership for a book of this nature is vast. In excess of 400 writers' circles meet regularly and at least 250 small press magazines are devoted to writing in one form or another. Five commercial magazines are devoted to freelance writing. Writing is a pastime to interest anyone of any age, social class or race. It is inexpensive to get started and offers the opportunity to earn income into the bargain.

Your proposal needs to have been well enough thought through for you to be able to say, within ten per cent or so, how long it is likely to be. You need to relay this length to the publisher so that it can make a judgement of where, if at all, it will fit into its publishing programme. Most publishers will be flexible on this point, bearing in mind the physical restraints of binding just a few pages to make them into a book. Rarely are works of less than 30,000 words ever published.

Whatever the proposed length of your book you need to show a flexible approach towards it. You could say something like:

> I envisage a length of 50,000 words to be appropriate to cover the subject of this book in the detail suitable for the area of

such a work. Having said that, I can be flexible in my approach and adjust the length should you have alternative views.

If you have gained some track record in the field of writing you can include details of your writing experience by way of a short outline. This need be only a paragraph or two. It can include titles of books, but it doesn't need to include reference to article titles.

You should only include commercial successes. Do not include anything you may have had published by a vanity publisher. This will impress no-one. Indeed, it is likely to have the reverse effect and possibly spoil any chance you may have had of creating a good impression. (We'll take a look at the vanity press in the next chapter.)

To give you a better idea here is my own outline of experience at the time of writing this book:

> I have had three books published: *How to Make Money Out of Writing* (Gower, 1989), *How to Win Consumer Competitions* (Kogan Page, 1992) and *The Dreamer's Guide to Winning the Big Competition Prizes* (Breese Books, 1995). I am currently under contract to write two more books: one for Allison and Busby and one for Century. I have also had six business handbooks published and over 300 articles and short stories which have appeared in more than fifty magazine titles ranging from *Rattlers Tale* to *Chat*, *Competitors Journal* to *Young Mother*. I have also taken part in radio and television programmes including the live shows *Woman's Hour* and *The Time, The Place*. I am a Member of The Society of Authors.

If you truly are a complete novice and have written nothing before, you are better off not trying to compile any experience profile at all. A list of near misses will impress no-one. You would be wiser to concentrate all effort on lifting the other elements of your proposal to as high a standard as possible. You could substitute details of your knowledge of the subject of the book in question.

The last element of your proposal should comprise the core of your book: the synopsis. This could be compiled in line with what we said in the last chapter.

If your work is unknown to your target publisher you should include a sample of the finished work, usually by way of a sample chapter or two. These needn't necessarily be the first two chapters, any two will do, just so long as they are representative of the work as a whole. The sample needn't be any more than about 5,000 words, just so long as it is sufficient for the publisher to determine that the style is right for the work in question. You have to demonstrate in this sample that you can write and get your ideas across in an interesting and entertaining way.

If you can get all the elements of your proposal across as outlined above you should be well on the way to securing a contract.

More About Timing

We covered, to some extent, the timing of submissions in chapter one – how to meet deadlines for commissioned work – but there are other occasions when you will need to consider timing of on-spec pieces as well. This is when writing seasonal or anniversary pieces. An article on Easter eggs submitted in April will arrive too late to be considered. The copy for an Easter edition of a monthly magazine could have been selected as early as January. It is therefore wise to plan ahead and submit these types of submission well in advance. I suggest the following to be the minimum lead times you should allow:

Weekly publications – 2 months
Monthly publications – 3 months
Quarterly publications – 6 months

Once you have despatched your masterpiece all you have to do is sit back and wait for the acceptance cheque to arrive. Or is it? Whilst it is nice to have such confidence in your abilities you can't always rely on others being so well organised. Some editors respond quickly to what they have been offered, some do not. This can cause problems if you are left to wonder whether you simply have a slow-coach editor on your hands, or whether your submission has gone astray in the post. The temptation is to telephone or write to enquire whether or not it has arrived. But you should resist over eagerness if you are to avoid irritating your target editor. I always leave it three months before querying weekly or monthly magazines and six months for quarterlies.

Multiple Submissions

A question frequently posed by newcomers to writing is: 'Can I submit the same piece of work simultaneously to two or more editors?' When it comes to short works the simple answer is: 'No.' Otherwise the magazine editor has no way of knowing whether he/she is free to use your offering. When you offer an article or a short story to a magazine it is assumed that the editor is free to publish the piece to suit its editorial timetable. That could be this week, next week, some time in the future, or maybe never. It has to be when and if a free space becomes available. If an editor hasn't that freedom, the piece is of little value. He/she will rarely purchase a work in the *hope* a space will become available. That space has to be available in the first place before a decision can be made. And when a decision has been made there is usually insufficient time to make an offer and for that offer to be accepted. The opportunity to fill the space will have passed. So the piece is used when needed and the author is paid at the magazine's 'usual rate'.

When it comes to book-length work the picture looks very different. An offer is *always* made before a book is published. The author is free to accept or decline that offer. So nothing is lost by multiple submissions. If more than one offer is made for the same piece of work the author simply accepts the best one and declines the other/s.

Despatching Work
Never staple a typescript. Short works should be secured with nothing more permanent than a paper clip. Full-length works should not be secured at all. Do not fold your work but mail it out flat. If you have included photographs or illustrations, protect them by use of a card-backed envelope.

Always include return postage. If you are submitting a short piece this can be by way of a stamped self-addressed envelope. For full-length works either include a label with sufficient stamps on it or include a cheque to cover the amount. If you are submitting work to an overseas publishing house, include sufficient International Reply Coupons to cover return postage.

When you get around to sending out your work, package it in such a way that it will look respectable by the time it reaches its destination. Provide sufficient protection to keep it neat. When sending out a full-length work, package it in a cardboard box and then wrap it in brown paper. Secure this with adhesive tape and string. Use only new packaging materials. Re-used paper and envelopes covered in correction fluid and masking tape never impressed anyone.

Earnings

Samuel Johnson once said: 'Sir, no one but a blockhead ever wrote except for money.' And he had a point. If a publisher considers your work good enough to print and make a profit from it, why shouldn't you share in that profit? Admittedly, the beginning writer's first ambition is simply to see work in print – but you should be sure this is achieved fairly. The newcomer to carpentry wouldn't expect not to be paid for a first satisfactory attempt at cabinet making. So why shouldn't the writer always be paid for early works too? Just for the satisfaction of seeing your work in print? No way! Resist any attempt by unscrupulous editors to obtain your work without fair recompense.

Having said that, you still need to be realistic about your

expectations. Whilst the rewards for writing can be high in terms of personal satisfaction they may not be so great in monetary terms, so don't overestimate what you can earn to begin with. Some beginning writers become so enthusiastic about their writing ambitions that they lose sight of reality. Writing is hard work, particularly at the beginning, and earnings can be slow to start coming in. Few new writers earn sufficient to make a living. My advice to the beginner is to repeat the cliché: 'Don't give up the day job.' At least not until you have begun to earn enough from your writing to be able to pay all of your normal household bills.

Rates of Pay
Fees for freelance writing in magazines can vary a great deal, depending largely on the circulation of the journals concerned. Sometimes, a well-known figure is able to command a higher fee than a beginner, but otherwise payment is much the same for everyone. Payment is usually made after publication but some journals pay on acceptance, which can, on occasion, be some time before publication, depending on lead times.

It is not possible in a book of this nature to give actual rates of pay for they can vary so greatly for the different publications available and can change suddenly according to market forces and to changes in publishing policy. The best place to look for guidance is in one of the yearbooks we outlined earlier. Suffice it to say the rate per thousand words can vary from the price of a meal out for some of the smaller circulation magazines to ten times this amount for some of the national glossies. Those wanting to aim high should go for magazines in the circulation group 'A' which adhere to the National Union of Journalists' (NUJ) rates. These rates can be obtained from one of the yearbooks or from the *Freelance Fees Guide* obtainable from the NUJ at:

National Union of Journalists,
Acorn House,
314 Gray's Inn Road,
London,
WC1X 8DP.

Royalties

Payment for books is usually by way of a royalty. This is usually calculated as a percentage of the retail price of copies sold. Sometimes though, royalties are based on net receipts, which is the publisher's *income* from the sale of books.

In the past The Society of Authors has warned against signing a contract that paid only against net receipts for you could never know what their likely income would be against a given print run. However, it seems that writers will have little choice in the future for we saw the end to the Net Book Agreement (NBA) in 1995.

The NBA was an agreement between publishers that they could choose to sell books at 'net' prices, which would ensure that booksellers would not sell these books at less than the 'net' price. Publishers did not have to publish under this agreement, but most did. Since the abolition of the NBA, booksellers have been able to sell at whatever price they like. It is now possible that publishers will be forced into selling quantities of books at such low prices that they can no longer guarantee in their contract with authors how much the author is to receive against each sale. The inclusion of a 'net receipts' clause therefore now seems likely. Time will tell.

Traditionally, the royalty on hardback books begins at 10% of the cover price. There will usually be a clause which will raise this percentage should the book sell above a specified volume. Typically, royalties on a hardback will be 10% on the first 2,500, 12½% on the next 2,500, and 15% on all copies sold thereafter. Fifteen per cent is normal when it comes to copies covered by the publisher's net receipts. However, the net receipt rate can be even lower (say, 10% of the publisher's net receipts when a particularly high discount is to be given, for example for a bookclub edition.

Paperback royalties are somewhat lower, normally starting at 7½% rising to 10% after the sale of 20,000 copies. Again, percentages will be lower for net receipts.

Royalty payment dates are sometimes provided for as little as once per year. You would be wise to seek a payment at least twice per annum, covering the first two years of publication.

Advances

It is usual in book contracts to include a clause which gives the author the right to receive certain advance payments against royalties yet to be earned. This is to cover the period during which the book is being written and whilst it is being produced before it appears in the shops. Otherwise a writer would need to spend a considerable time producing the book during which he/she would receive no income.

The time at which advances are paid varies from one contract to another, but typically it will be half on delivery of the manuscript, and the other half on the date of publication. For previously published authors it can be half on signing the contract and half on delivery of the manuscript.

Bear in mind that these payments are only an advance on royalties. In other words, it is the publisher's assessment of the minimum royalties your book is likely to earn. If sales fail to reach this figure then you will never see any further royalty payments. If it is in excess of this figure, then of course further royalties will be paid in accordance with the percentage terms of the agreement.

The size of advance will vary greatly from one publishing house to another and from one author to another. An unknown author will command perhaps a few hundred pounds – maybe a thousand if he/she is lucky, whereas the Jeffrey Archers of the writing world can command hundreds of thousands of pounds. It all depends on the publisher's expectations of sales. Typically, advances are calculated at two-thirds of the royalties of the entire first print run of the book, calculated at cover price, but this is by no means always the case. Sometimes, the expected income for high discount sales is also taken into consideration.

Kill Fees

When a magazine offers to buy an article at an agreed rate for payment on publication it does so in the belief that it will be able to use the piece. It is the normal course of events for the article to be published and the author to receive the associated fee on time. However, occasions do sometimes arise when the accepted article isn't used. This can be for all manner of reasons resulting in a change of editorial policy, such as new ownership or a new person taking over the editorial chair. This is effectively a breach of contract which needs to be addressed. Usually, this is done by way of a 'kill fee', which is a fee paid in compensation. If the piece is particularly topical where it would easily lose its saleability beyond a given period of time, then the fee paid is usually the full amount. However, this fee is usually lower than the fee that would have been paid had the piece been used, for it does leave the author free to offer the First British Serial Rights elsewhere. As this means you can effectively earn two fees for the same piece, not too many authors complain about such an arrangement.

Public Lending Right

Public Lending Right (PLR) was set up by the Government in 1979 as the result of pressure from authors and interested associations such as The Society of Authors and The Writers Guild of Great Britain. Now, Parliament allocates a sum of money each year to pay for the scheme, which ensures that the author is paid a fee every time a book is borrowed from a public library. That fee varies according to the size of the PLR fund and to the number of borrowings in any one year. Loans are monitored every 12 months over the period 1st July to 30th June.

The Registrar of the PLR scheme keeps records of all loans from a selection of public libraries. These libraries are spread throughout England, Scotland, Wales and Northern Ireland. This record is used to average out and to estimate the total loans from libraries throughout the country. In order to avoid the possibility of unrepresentative patterns developing to distort the figures, no library can stay in the sample for more than four years.

An annual statement of estimated loans is issued by the Registrar of the scheme to every registered author, and payment is made once a year, in February. There is a ceiling to PLR in any one year, the amount of which varies from time to time to prevent top-selling writers receiving too much. Also, if a book has so few borrowings that its earnings would amount to less than a set limit, then the author is paid nothing.

In order to benefit from the scheme, the author must apply for registration and certain criteria have to be met to establish him/her as the author. In the PLR system you are the author of a book if you are the writer, illustrator, translator, compiler, editor or reviser, provided your name is mentioned on the title page. Co-authorship is covered by the scheme and each co-author/illustrator can receive a share of the PLR earnings provided there are no more than three of them. Each must specify at the time of registration what percentage share of the proceeds each should receive.

An author's first application for PLR must be made out on a comprehensive form (FAR) which must be counter-signed by an MP, lawyer, doctor, bank official, minister of religion or other professional person who has been known to the author for at least two years. Subsequent books may be registered on a simpler form (SAR) requiring no counter-signature.

A PLR application form can be obtained from:

Public Lending Right Office,
Bayheath House,
Prince Regent Street,
Stockton on Tees,
Cleveland,
TS18 1DF.

Rejection

The odds of having any of your work published are stacked against you. The competition is fierce and consequently only a small proportion of work offered for sale ever finds its way into print. You have to be philosophical about this fact. You need to tell yourself, and be convinced, that your work is better than anyone else's and so it will constantly be within that small percentage that gets published. Have no time for negative thinking.

Take a look at some famous writers to see how they suffered rejection upon rejection before the publishing world took notice of their talent. Lewis Carroll's classic *Alice in Wonderland* was rejected so often he ended up paying to have it published himself. So too, did JRR Tolkien with his *Lord of the Rings*. One publisher told Richard Adams that his *Watership Down* was 'too solemn, babyish, and its language too difficult'. Three other publishers must have had similar thoughts for they too failed to comprehend how adults could possibly gain enjoyment from reading a book about rabbits. And what about poor old John Creasy? He is said to have collected 968 rejection slips before having his work accepted. And he went on to write an impressive list of novels.

You have to think of all the rejections you receive as part of the learning process. You need to realise that every rejection you receive is part of that process and each one brings you another step closer to an acceptance.

In common with many accomplishments in life, successful freelance writing is largely a question of attitude. Those who believe in themselves and write positively and with enthusiasm undoubtedly stand a better chance of getting published than those who simply dabble at it.

Set your standards high and keep writing. Once something is in the mail, begin something new. Forget your last submission and think of your next attempt. Keep up the pressure all the time – a winning attitude wins acceptances.

6

Publishing

Commercial Publishing

When you write a book which is accepted by a commercial publisher you will be offered a written contract. This contract will state the terms and conditions under which you will write the book. This will give the rate per copy sold at which you will be paid and what you are expected to produce in return for this payment.

In general, you will be expected to produce the manuscript, plus, if relevant, any illustrations required, an index, and all necessary permissions.

If illustrations are required the contract will clearly state that it will be your responsibility to produce them. If you are unable to do this for yourself it will be your responsibility to pay someone else to produce them for you. On rare occasions the publisher will provide some illustrations, but these would be at your cost.

Under normal circumstances you will be expected to provide your own index. If you are unable (or unwilling) to do so the publisher will offer to employ a professional indexer to produce it for you, but this too will be at your cost.

If you have quoted from the copyright material in your book it will be your responsibility to obtain, and to pay for, any permissions required in this respect. Normally, you will also be required to provide your publisher with written evidence of these permissions.

Apart from these exceptions, it would be unusual for a commercial publisher to ask you to fund anything else, except your incidental expenses such as some paper and some ink, and perhaps some expenses for research, such as bus fares to your local library or some postage stamps for letters. Other than this you normally pay for nothing. The cost of typesetting, printing, warehousing, distribution and sales, will all be the responsibility of the publisher.

Self-publishing

Sometimes an author will decide to produce a book at his/her own expense. There can be several reasons for this. Probably the most common reason is that an author has made many attempts to sell a work to a commercial publisher but has failed to find a buyer. In these circumstances the work can simply be abandoned or the author can elect to publish it for him/herself, particularly if the author has continued faith in the value of the work.

Another common reason for self-publishing is the knowledge that the work has no commercial chance because it is of limited appeal. The autobiography of Fred Smith the milkman covering his experiences of 30 years as a roundsman is unlikely to command a wide audience. Unless, of course, he has become famous for some other reason, such as having won the lottery in a big way or having married a film star. But under normal circumstances no-one would be interested in reading about such a person and so no publisher would entertain publishing it.

Both of these examples are valid reasons for self-publishing a work just so long as the author is fully aware of what is involved and how much he/she is likely to get out of the necessary capital expenditure.

To be a self-publisher you need to be a great deal more than just an author. You need to take on, or at least co-ordinate, all of the roles the commercial publisher takes on. This can be both an expensive and stressful experience.

Given a little time for research most authors should be able to obtain estimates for the necessary production of the book. This process alone is enough to put many writers off though, for the expense of printing say, one thousand copies, would amount to several thousand pounds.

Let us say that costs so far are insufficient deterrent. What happens after your book has been printed and bound and delivered en masse to your doorstep? Well, you need to sell it. But to whom? You are completely unknown to the book trade so what bookseller would be interested in buying your book for resale? You have no credentials. You could send out some advertising flyers to book shops – several thousand of them – but no prizes for guessing how many orders you are likely to receive. You could try some personal visits to improve your chances of a few sales, but how many book shops can you hope to visit by yourself?

You could, of course, concentrate on consumers that have an interest in the theme of your book. If you have written a book about fishing rods you could advertise in some angling magazines. Or you could buy a targeted mailing list from a specialist direct mail house in an effort to win some orders. Some individuals do make a profit from self-publishing but they have to work very hard at it.

If you are convinced self-publishing may be an option for you, further investigation is recommended by reading a copy of Harry Mulholland's book entitled *Guide to Self-Publishing* (ISBN 0 9507121 4 0) published by – you've guessed it – the author himself. The address is:

Mulholland-Wirral,
The Croft,
School Avenue,
Little Neston,
South Wirral,
L64 4BS.

Subsidy Publishing

What is a subsidy publisher?

A subsidy publisher declares that it is a body that will produce an author's book on a shared cost basis. The publisher will put up part of the cost and the author will put up the other part (or so it is said). The reason for this is quite simple. Publishing is a risky business; costs are high and profits often low. Whilst many books that are offered to subsidy publishers are of undoubted literary merit (they say) they can have limited market potential and so publishing them would put these companies at financial risk. In these circumstances it is proposed that publisher and author share the risk of publication. This is what most 'subsidy' publishers say of themselves – or something very similar.

If you haven't heard this scenario before it demands some of your attention for it could cost a great deal of your hard earned cash if you are unfortunate enough to get caught up in it.

Let's get back to the original question of what constitutes a subsidy publisher. The answer is quite simple. A subsidy publisher is nothing more than a vanity publisher. It just sounds better to be called a subsidy publisher.

Vanity Publishing

OK, so a subsidy publisher is really a vanity publisher; what then does a vanity publisher do? The truthful answer may sound cynical, but it is not. What a vanity publisher actually does is: not a lot. And charges a great deal of money for it.

Let's take a look at how a vanity publisher operates. Perhaps you have seen their advertisements in the national press. Invariably they begin on inviting lines: 'Publisher seeks authors. If you have written a book that deserves publication write to . . .', 'Book publisher seeks authors . . .', 'Authors – sympathetic publisher would like to hear from you . . .', 'Authors in search of a publisher should contact . . .'. All of these are actual examples of advertisements. Often they continue on from their opening lines by asking the reader to submit a manuscript for appraisal. Not unnaturally, such talk can sound attractive if you have been hiking your book around the publishing scene without success.

In response to the replies generated by these advertisements, the vanity publisher despatches a glowing report on *every* manuscript it receives (irrespective of merit) together with the company's sales literature. Praise for every book is beyond all expectation – they are all works of true brilliance.

Overall, the sales blurb from these companies varies somewhat but the core message is the same. It usually goes something like this: If you have spent months/years writing your book, and have then sent your precious manuscript around the publishers to no avail, you can either forget your hard work and let it gather dust, or you can let us help. You have to realise though, that publishing is a hazardous business, particularly with an unpublished author. Production costs are high and so inevitably risks are high. It is therefore proposed that author and publisher work together as a partnership and share the cost of publication.

By way of compensation the author will be paid a much higher royalty than publishing by traditional methods. This way if the book sells well the author's reward will be that much greater. Of course, the publisher cannot risk this share of the investment unless it is at first convinced the book has a reasonable chance of success. But yours has a good chance of such achievement.

Remember too, that your rewards will go beyond financial considerations; think of the wider recognition and greater prestige your book will generate. Think of the many famous authors you will join as having contributed towards the publication of their work: Byron, Browning, Shelley, Tennyson, Gray, Kipling, Pope, Poe.

Once the book has been printed and bound the author will be sent six copies free of charge; and then sales promotion will get under way. Promotion will usually be by the sending out of review copies of the book to newspapers and magazines; the author's local book shops; local libraries. In addition, copies of a sales leaflet will be sent to leading wholesalers, and libraries nationwide. Copies of the book will also be sent to Whitakers for entry in their lists in *The Bookseller* and *Books in Print*.

All of this can sound very promising to the eager new author, but you would do well to analyse just what you are going to get before parting with your cash. In most cases the offer consists of the delivery to the author of a limited quantity of the bound book (usually six), plus promotion and royalties on sales. And that doesn't amount to much. After you have received your personal copies of the book (usually 18 months or so after you have signed the contract and parted with your cash) you will undoubtedly be faced with stony silence. A further six months goes by. A year. Still nothing.

You write to the publisher enquiring after your royalities. The reply is despondent: 'Despite the remarkable standard of your manuscript sales have not met expectations and the reserve quantity of books sold before royalties can be paid has yet to be realised. Perhaps next year . . .' But next year comes and the result is the same. The reserve never is met. All you have seen for your money are your personal copies of the bound volume.

In truth, the lack of success of the venture can be measured by taking a look at that one fundamental: 'promotion'. Vanity press imprints have become well known to the trade so their proposed sales methods are on shaky ground from just one principle: the authorship standard from one book to another will vary greatly and so the prospective outlet can never be sure of the quality of any one particular book. So the buyer doesn't take any of them. And unless the end product is presented to the public for consideration it will be unaware of its existence – a situation hardly likely to generate sales. The proposed marketing strategy simply cannot work.

Vanity publishing is expensive – a 'contribution' by the author of several thousand pounds is not uncommon. So unless you want to effectively pay hundreds of pounds for each of the personal copies of your book you shouldn't enter into a subsidy or vanity publishing agreement.

Remember, a reputable commercial publisher will *never* ask you to pay for publication. If your book is worth publishing the publisher will undertake the venture entirely at its own risk.

Contracts

A contract is an agreement between two parties which is enforceable by law. When you are dealing with short works such as puzzles, articles and short stories, that contract usually consists of a letter or an exchange of letters. When it comes to a book-length work a more formal contract is nearly always agreed by the parties involved.

Many new authors are so excited at the receipt of a contract that they sign it without a moment's thought. This impulse should be resisted. Publishers' agreements, as the phrase implies, are compiled by publishers, which sometimes means they can be loaded in the publishers' favour. It is therefore essential to read an agreement carefully to ensure you understand it and to ensure you can fulfil your end of the deal. If you can get the contract checked by an experienced body such as a lawyer, The Society of Authors, or your agent (if you have one), so much the better.

The possible variations in book publishing contracts are vast and no single set of guidelines could cover all potential clauses, but here we'll take a look at those you are most likely to come across, but not in any particular order of importance.

Publishers' Agreements

The contract will identify the work that is to be written and the parties covered by it: the publisher and the author/s. This will also identify how the work is to appear: in hardcover and/or paperback. It is common today for books, both fiction and non-fiction to be published direct into paperback without first being published in hardback. Most new writers won't have too much to say about the form in which their book is to appear, they will normally be content that it is to appear in print at all. There is nothing wrong with this position, of course, but sometimes authors can have reservations that their work is to appear in paperback without first having been aired in hardcover. If, for example, a work is to have many quality illustrations you may have strong views that they should be displayed in hardcover to show them off to proper advantage. In this case you need to ask yourself if the alternative is acceptable for it could be that if you don't accept a paperback version the work may not be published at all.

We have already said it is unwise to part with the copyright to your work and the reasons why this is so. Fortunately though, it is usual in a book contract for the publisher to purchase only the volume rights and certain other subsidiary and ancillary rights, so the question of parting with copyright rarely arises. The royalty system is the most frequently adopted form of agreement for all book-length works. This gives the publisher the exclusive right to print and sell your book in whatever country or countries the contract specifies. Film and other rights for a non-fiction book are seldom worth worrying about, but if you have written a novel you should ensure that it provides for a fair system of payment for other rights. Typically, your earnings from these would be split 50/50 with the publisher. Also ensure that if electronic rights are included you don't sign them away for no fee or royalty.

The contract will set a deadline for the completion and delivery of your manuscript which will have been mutually agreed. There could be penalties included in the contract if you fail to deliver by this date, including the clause that the publisher may refuse to go ahead and publish. You should ensure that you are happy you have sufficient time to write the book, including all necessary re-writes needed to bring it up to publishing standard. Think hard before signing, for it is a major commitment. Have you left yourself enough time to undertake all the tasks necessary? Research, writing, typing, checking, correcting, copying . . . And don't forget an allowance for colds and flu'. Publishers, like all business people, like to deal with dependable associates. Having said that, hopefully they are also realists, so if something really unexpected does happen to prevent you from meeting your deadline, such as serious ill health, earthquake or flood, advise your publisher as soon as possible that you are unable to meet the contract date. If you really have got a legitimate reason for failing to meet your commitment, it is likely the publisher will have a sympathetic attitude.

The contract will specify an approximate number of words. As we said earlier, you should already have debated this aspect of your book with the publisher at enquiry stage and agreed a suitable length. It is best to stick to this as near as you possibly can for it is likely this will play an important part in the book's costings and cover price.

If you will be using illustrations check your contract carefully as your payment for the reproduction fees might be more than you would earn in royalties. Under these circumstances a separate picture budget is sometimes allocated. Also, with children's books, the illustrator is often appointed by the publisher.

If you are to use any copyright material take note of who will be responsible for obtaining permissions. As we have said already, this is almost certainly to be your responsibility.

Non-fiction works often contain an index. Where this is the case, it is normally the author's responsibility to provide it. The author may elect for the publisher to have it undertaken on his/her behalf and the cost of preparation deducted from the author's royalties.

Once you have completed your work and submitted it, the publisher will have the book typeset. Copies of the proofs will then be sent to you for checking. You need to read through them to ensure they are an accurate translation of your typescript. If there are any mistakes you will have to mark them up for correction. It should be noted that this is for the purpose of identifying typesetting errors only and not an opportunity to re-write any of your script that you no longer feel happy with. The contract will reserve the right of the publisher to charge you for any alterations of your own if these amount to more than a certain percentage (15% is usual) of the total cost of typesetting. And you will almost certainly be charged the full cost of any alterations to illustrations.

Many contracts require the author to revise the work for any new edition. Under normal circumstances you should have no objections to such a clause. Indeed, you should insist on a work being revised if your reputation is likely to suffer because circumstances have changed which make your book inaccurate. Topical material, for example, can become out-of-date. However, if the scope of such revision is extensive (say in excess of 10% of the text) you should seek recompense for undertaking this work.

It is common for book contracts to include a clause that entitles the author to receive on publication a certain number of free copies of the work. Very often this number is six, but few publishers would refuse if you asked for this to be increased to, say, ten copies. I have had as many as 20 copies. This clause will also state that you will be at liberty to purchase further copies, for personal use, on trade terms. These will, in fact, be cheaper than they appear, because you will be credited with your usual royalties on these.

Contracts always contain warranties and indemnity clauses. These state that the author is entitled to enter into an agreement to write the work for the publisher and that it has not been published before. It will also stress that all of the author's statements purporting to be facts are true. The work must not contain anything libellous, obscene, in breach of duty of confidence or in any other way unlawful or illegal. This will include a clause which states that the work does not infringe an existing copyright. Only the author can know whether or not he/she can sign such a statement in all honesty.

Ensure that the contract specifies that you are to be offered first refusal of all outstanding copies of the work when they are to be remaindered. A book is usually offered at a very low lump sum price for all remaining copies when ordinary sales have fallen to an uneconomic level. The author should always be given the first opportunity to purchase these, usually for resale with the associated profits therefore going to themselves. An author usually takes up this offer when he/she is confident that he/she has sufficient contacts to be able to market them all, such as at functions where there are book signings.

Ensure that the contract does not attempt to write out your moral rights as covered by the 1988 Copyright Act (see Chapter 3 for details).

Many contracts include an option clause which requires the author to offer his/her next work to the same publisher. If a publisher spends a great deal of money on advertising a first book and so establishing the author's reputation, an option clause seems only fair and there can be little harm in it in principle provided the time required to make a decision on the work is specified and is of a short duration (typically four weeks). It would however, be foolish to commit yourself to publish another work on the same terms. It should be made clear that if the publisher does not take up the option in your next book you would be free to offer it elsewhere.

The publisher will insist (not unreasonably) that the author shall not be allowed to publish with another publisher a book which is virtually an abridged or expanded version of the work. However, you should analyse the wording of such a clause to ensure that it is not *so* restrictive that it prevents the writing of genuinely different works.

Contracts always have clauses dealing with advances and royalties, both of which we covered in the last chapter.

The Minimum Terms Agreement

The Minimum Terms Agreement (MTA) first appeared in 1980. This was drawn up jointly by The Society of Authors and The Writer's Guild of Great Britain. It is a document which has been signed by both of these organisations and a particular publishing house. There are various MTAs with several publishers, and they are all different.

An agreement effectively guarantees that an author will get a fair deal, not just on financial matters but in terms of consultation, for example on when the book will be published and what it will look like.

A MTA will only be offered, in usual circumstances, to either a member of The Society of Authors or The Writer's Guild of Great Britain. Very often these days though, publishers who have signed such an agreement will offer all their authors a MTA.

There are some types of book to which the MTA does not apply. These are books where illustrations take up 40% or more of the space; specialist works on the visual arts where illustrations fill 25% or more of the space; books involving three or more participants in the royalties; and technical books, manuals and reference books.

7

Organisations for Writers

Are writers born or are they made? Is commercial literacy simply a gift, or can it be learned in the same way one learns to ride a bicycle? As I've already said, I believe it can be learned. But there is a body of opinion in writing circles which says either you can write or you cannot. Doris Lessing once said: 'If you are a writing person, you write. If you are a painter, you paint.' But I doubt this can be correct thinking. By this yardstick, if you are a criminal person, you rob banks. I believe it to be attitude that decides what we do and how well we do it. If you want something badly enough, usually you can fight to get it.

But if writing can be learned as I suggest, by which teaching method is it best for the aspiring writer to study?

Writing schools

Many apprentice freelance writers attempt to learn their craft via a correspondence course. And this is fine, so long as you treat such courses flexibly. (And if you can afford the fees.)

Whenever you read articles about how professional writers set about their work, the one thing to be learned is that no two authors approach their writing in exactly the same way. Indeed, one approach can often be opposite to another.

There are those established writers of fiction, for example, who work out an entire plot before they can begin to think of writing their story. Each chapter has to be outlined, complete with the characters that are to appear and the role each is to play. Without a firm framework, they maintain, the finished work is likely to be thin and unbelievable. You have to have a solid base upon which to build your work. John Braine, for one, has said he makes a chapter-by-chapter outline of a novel before he begins to write.

Other writers maintain they haven't a clue what is going to happen until they have written it. Stan Barstow doesn't have an outline before he begins to write. He has said: 'I start a novel with much less than this [an outline] and do my thinking on paper.' Novelist Terence Feely maintains: 'You don't necessarily have to know every detail of your plot before you start.'

Such writers often start with a vague idea in mind then sit down, either with a sheet of paper and a pen in hand, or at their keyboard, and simply begin to write. As they go they let each situation build upon the preceding page until their story is finished. This technique inevitably involves the author in a considerable amount of rewriting, but for some it is the only way they can work.

There are those, too, who use both techniques or a combination of both. With so many divergent approaches (all of which are successful for respective individuals) it must be difficult for writing schools to attempt to teach any one particular approach. How can they know which will appeal to any one student?

Some writing schools try to reduce the art of fiction writing to formula: how to undertake plotting; characterisation; setting; themes; choice of viewpoint. In my experience this cannot be a successful approach. Twenty-five years ago I took a correspondence course in creative writing which attempted to employ this technique; it took a number of years to unlearn what I had been taught. And it was only then, after I had started to write what came naturally (without confining 'rules') that I attained editorial acceptance.

Not everyone would agree with me, of course. The results of a survey I once undertook would bear this out. Comments about different writing schools from various ex-students ranged from 'Years out of date' and 'Boring' to 'Marvellous' and 'Excellent'. The survey revealed that roughly half the students were happy with what they received for their money and half were not. This seems to me to be rather a high risk for those contemplating a course, particularly as they can cost a couple of hundred pounds and more. For this, students usually receive a set of written material as well as tutorial comments on their work. The quality of both seemed to vary greatly; written material was either 'Clear and detailed' or 'Pre-printed . . . very boring', and the tutorial comments either 'Excellent' or 'Awful'.

Before starting on a writing course you would do well to ask yourself what you expect to gain from it. If you need to learn the basic mechanics of writing: elementary plot development, pointers to characterisation, subject-matter for articles, market research, manuscript presentation, etc, then a course may be just what you need. But don't expect to find a magic formula for success. Bear in mind the words of Barbara Taylor Bradford: 'I truly believe that learning the craft of fiction writing is vital and that you can't do that at classes.' Or Terence Feely, who maintains: 'There is no point in discussing with anyone the art of characterisation or construction or dialogue. If they are writers, they will know, even though it will take them time to achieve what they know.'

So, if you do go to a writing school, particularly one that offers a set 'method', treat what you are taught flexibly. Write the way you want to write, not how you think others would write. Above all, bear in mind that there can be no substitute for the actual process of writing itself.

Having said all that, the same can be said of all teaching methods. You are after all reading a book which hopefully will help you to learn to write. But a book costs just a few pounds. Writing courses cost a great deal more. It's all a question of getting value for money.

There are many writing schools to choose from, but here is a random sample of three:

International Correspondence Schools,
312/314 High Street,
Sutton,
Surrey,
SM1 1PR.

Writers' Craft,
29 Turnpike Lane,
London,
N8 0EP.

Writers News Limited,
Home Study Divison,
PO Box 4,
Nairn,
Scotland,
IV12 4HU.

Adult education courses

Much of what we said of correspondence courses applies to adult education classes. Except that writing can be learned for much less money by this method. Evening classes can cost as little as a few pounds per term.

Another point in favour of local authority evening classes is that you can benefit from their personal approach. If you have a query on a lesson of a correspondence course you have to wait for an exchange of letters to gain an answer. And even then it may not be an answer that is lucid to you. Evening classes, on the other hand, offer immediate answers to questions.

The value of local classes depends, of course, on the ability of the tutor taking the class. This can vary from one school to another. For the newcomer to writing however, most will be of some value in getting started.

Evening courses also give you the opportunity to mingle with others having the same writing aspirations as yourself. Some who attend classes do so more for the sake of a pleasant evening amongst other writers than for the instruction.

Local authority evening classes usually begin in September, so the associated prospectus for these is available in July. Usually, these are to be found at your local library. Lists of contact numbers for courses are also often to be found in your local newspaper or free sheet. Finally, you can obtain information on where to find details of courses from your local council offices.

Writers' circles

As with evening classes, many aspiring authors find congenial company in attending writers' circles, only perhaps more so. They tend to be more informal and relaxed and so it is easier to make friends and join in the conversation.

Some circles are run on more formal lines than others. A programme of lectures is often arranged coupled with the reading of new work by the assembled members. Readings are often followed by a criticism session which can be invaluable in steering a piece to publishing standard. You will not have to be too thin-skinned at such sessions though. Otherwise you could find yourself offended by what others say of your masterly prose. Other circles tend to be far less formal, with chatter of literary successes and failures over cups of coffee or tea. The only way to find a circle to suit you is to try some until you find one you feel comfortable with.

Many circles are run free of charge by different members offering their homes on a rota basis, whereas others which are run on a more formal basis at a village hall will charge a small membership fee.

A directory of writers' circles has been published by Laurence Pollinger Limited. This is arranged alphabetically and lists writers' circles and similar groups meeting regularly in the United Kingdom and Eire. All those listed welcome new members and each entry names a contact so prospective members may locate circles in their locality and obtain further information. The directory can be obtained from its compiler, Jill Dick, at:

Oldacre,
Horderns Park Road,
Chapel-en-le-Frith,
Derbyshire,
SK12 6SY.

The Society of Authors

The Society was founded in 1884 and is still going strong today. It is an independent trade union and offers its members support and guidance on matters of authorship. It advises on negotiations with publishers, broadcasting organisations, theatre managers and film companies. It also takes up complaints on any issue concerned with the business of authorship and can pursue legal actions for breach of contract or copyright infringement.

Its aims are to promote the interests of authors and to defend their rights. The society campaigns for the benefit of the profession in many ways. It negotiates improved terms and conditions (the Society and The Writers' Guild of Great Britain have a number of minimum terms agreements with publishers). It lobbies MPs, ministers and government departments for new legislation. It promotes the interests of specialist writers. There are groups within the Society for broadcasters, children's writers and illustrators, educational writers, medical writers and translators. The Society also litigates in matters of importance to writers.

In addition to these benefits the Society publishes the quarterly journal *The Author*.

There are four regional groups, each of which hold regular meetings. These are: The Society of Authors in Scotland, Authors North, East Anglian Writers and Isle of Man Authors.

At the time of writing the Society had over 5,700 members, representative of all the media.

There are two categories of membership. Full Membership is for authors who have had a full-length work published (not at the author's expense), broadcast, or performed commercially in this country or who have an established reputation in another medium (eg, journalism). Associate Membership is for authors who have received an offer to publish or broadcast a full-length work or who publish their own work as a profit-making enterprise; and authors who have had occasional items broadcast or performed, or translation, articles, illustrations or short stories published. Full details of membership can be obtained from:

The Membership Secretary,
The Society of Authors,
84 Drayton Gardens,
London,
SW10 9SB.

The Writers' Guild of Great Britain

The Writers' Guild was founded in 1959 and is a trade union affiliated to the TUC. It aims to negotiate industrial agreements with publishing houses and in film, television, radio and theatre. It gives members advice on contractual problems in all aspects of their business life, and improves the status of the writer in Great Britain. In its day to day work the Guild takes up problems on behalf of individual members, gives advice on contracts, and helps with any problems which affect the life of its members as professional writers. The Guild is in constant touch with government and national institutions wherever and whenever the interests of the writer are in question or are being discussed.

The Guild publishes *The Writers' Newsletter* six times a year, keeping members in touch with current work and negotiations. The newsletter carries articles, letters and reports from members.

Membership is open to writers who have made a sale of work for television, film, theatre, radio or books. It organises meetings and events, and regular craft meetings are held by the Guild's specialist committees in television and film, radio, theatre, books, women's writing. Craft meetings provide the opportunity to meet those who control, work within or affect their sphere of writing. Members are mailed at least once a month with details of craft meetings, and with details of the latest agreements the guild has made. Full details of membership can be obtained from:

The Membership Officer,
The Writers' Guild of Great Britain,
430 Edgware Road,
London,
W2 1EH.

The National Union of Journalists

The NUJ is a trade union representing journalists throughout the UK, the Republic of Ireland, Paris, Brussels and Geneva. It represents writers, reporters, researchers, columnists, photographers, reviewers, picture researchers, editors, sub-editors, artists, copy editors, cartoonists, illustrators, designers, broadcasters, presenters, scriptwriters, producers, proof-readers, indexers, press officers, copywriters, public relations officers.

It offers its members many benefits including: advice and legal help; assistance when eliciting fees from reluctant payers; assistance in gaining work; a NUJ Press Card; advice on the protection of copyright; assistance in locating a suitable accountant; advice on suitable computer equipment, defence of the writer's rights. It also keeps writers in touch with each other.

The NUJ publishes: their official organ *The Journalist, Freelance Directory, Freelance Fees Guide* and policy pamphlets.

Membership is open to working journalists and at the time of writing it had 28,000 members. Full details can be obtained from:

The National Union of Journalists,
Acorn House,
314 Gray's Inn Road,
London,
WC1N 8DP.

8

Financial Affairs

Book-keeping

It is essential for the writer to keep accurate records, in two areas:

- Work which is on offer and to whom
- Details of all income and expenditure

The first of these records is necessary to enable you to keep track of what work is on offer, what has been accepted and therefore cannot be offered again, and what has been rejected and still needs a target to aim at.

The second of these is necessary to keep your bank account in order and to ensure you can keep the Inland Revenue happy.

Where Is It?

The simplest way to keep track of where your work is, is to compile a record sheet containing the following information:

- The identity of the piece of work
- To whom that work has been offered and when
- The outcome of each offer (whether accepted or rejected)
- By whom the piece was finally published and when
- The fee received and when.

Title	Offered to:				Accepted	Fee
Moving Pictures	Wealth Report 1/3/96				Wealth Report 15/3/96	Received 5/4/96
Take A Card	Wealth Report 1/3/96				Wealth Report 15/3/96	Received 5/4/96
The Making of Mail Order	Escape ® 8/3/96	Profit 22/2/96			Profit 19/4/96	Received 20/4/96
New Targets	Springboard 18/3/96				Springboard 29/3/96	Received 29/3/96
Hungry for Business	Profit 5/4/96				Profit 28/4/96	Received 2/5/96
The Filler Market (1)	F.W.&P. 12/4/96				F.W.&P. 27/4/96	Received 4/5/96
Dealth Plus	Profit 20/4/96				Profit 17/5/96	Received 24/5/96
More New Outlets	Springboard 25/4/96				Springboard 16/5/96	Received 24/5/96
Filler Markets (2)	F.W.&P. 9/5/96					
My Operation	Take A Break 17/5/96					
A Bookmaker's Profit	Escape 22/5/96					

Fig 7. An example of a work submission sheet.

I use one of these sheets for each type of submission: article, short story, filler, etc. All of the information needed can be contained on one side of A4 paper. For a typical submission sheet see *Fig 7*. This sheet needs to be divided into seven columns. In the first column you can enter the identity of the piece (its title). The following four columns can be used to enter where the work has been offered. The first of these columns is for the original target publication. If the work is not accepted by that market enter an 'R' (for 'rejected') in that column and move on to the next column with the follow-up market, and so on. The sixth column is to enter who has accepted the piece and when. The seventh column is to enter the fee received and when. This column can be used to monitor cash flow. If you haven't received payment within a reasonable period of the piece being published (say, within two months) you need to write to the publication concerned with a gentle reminder. If you haven't already submitted an invoice this is the time to do so. This is usually sufficient to jog memories and to elicit a response. All your invoice needs to give is your address and that of the addressee, plus the date (as in a letter) followed by something like this:

INVOICE No 001

First British Serial Rights in an article of 1,000 words entitled *The Best of Friends* for an agreed fee of £100, published in *Good Looks* on 1st July 1996.

If the work was commissioned and you included an invoice with your submission you need to write a letter. This needs to be short and to the point:

On 1st July 1996 you published my article *The Best of Friends* in your magazine *Good Looks*. This was covered by my invoice numbered 001, but to date I have not received payment. I would be grateful if you would expedite matters. Many thanks.

If a letter still doesn't elicit payment you should ring the accounts department of the magazine concerned. If you are still left out of pocket you need to ask yourself if the fee is worth further effort to chase. If it is, you could resort to the Small Claims Court, or if you are a member of The Society of Authors or The Writers' Guild you could enlist their help.

You also need to go through your submission sheet regularly (say once per week) to check outstanding editorial decisions. If you haven't heard anything for a while (three months for weeklies and monthlies, and six months for quarterlies) send a polite letter to the editor. Something like this:

> On 1st July 1996 I offered for your consideration a 1,000 word article entitled *The Best of Friends*. As I've not heard from you perhaps you would be kind enough to let me know whether or not you received the piece, and if so whether or not it is still under consideration. A SAE is enclosed for your reply.
> Many thanks.

You will not receive acceptance letters or rejection notices for everything you submit, of course. You couldn't expect an editor to respond to every readers' letter, for example. The only way you will know if a filler has been accepted is when it appears in print or when the payment for it arrives. This leaves you with the dilemma of not knowing whether a piece has been discarded or whether you simply have a slow-coach editor on your hands. So how long should you wait before you can safely assume your work is going to be used and therefore leaving you free to offer it elsewhere? Well, there is no guaranteed, fail safe rule, of course, but it should be sufficient to allow six months for weeklies and monthlies, and twelve months for quarterlies.

Financial Accounts
Keeping track of income and expenditure needn't be compli- cated. Indeed, it is best if it is quite straightforward. All you need

is some way of recording the money you earn from writing and the expenses you have to pay out in order to earn that income. The simplest way to keep track of these payments is by way of an analysis book.

Fig. 8 shows one page of such a book giving the headings I use for my accounting system. The first column simply gives the date when money was either received or expended. The second column gives brief details of that income and expenditure. The third column is for the entry of all income received. The remaining six columns are for all expenses incurred in undertaking the business of writing. Expenditure is broken down into columns like this to enable them to be totalled separately for the purpose of presenting accounts to the Inland Revenue.

Income Tax

Lord Thomas R. Duwar once said: 'The one thing that hurts more than paying an income tax is not having to pay an income tax.' The man had a point. Whilst it is irksome to have to share your good fortune with the Inland Revenue, you at least are in the happy position of earning an income to be able to pay income tax. You must be doing something right. And, contrary to popular belief, tax inspectors are usually helpful and co-operative people. So long as you present your accounts in an honest and straightforward manner they should present you with no great difficulty.

To begin with, when it is likely your writing output will be relatively small, you will probably be assessed under Case VI of Schedule D of the Income and Corporation Taxes Act 1988. In this case bona fide business expenses can be deducted in arriving at taxable income, but, if your expenses exceed your income, your loss can only be set against the profit from future isolated transactions, or other income assessable under Case VI.

Once you have gained some experience and your output has increased it may be possible to argue that, while your writing may be part-time, it is a profession nonetheless. In this case you will be

Date	Details	Receipts	Post	Research	Stationery	Travel	Subs	Other
20/4/96	Pay for "Making of M.O."	40-00						
1/5/96	Stamps: 20 @ 25p		5-00					
	20 @ 19p		3-80					
1/5/96	Glue stick				0-89			
2/5/96	Pay for "Hungry for Russia"	40-00						
6/5/96	Pay for "Take A Card"	40-00						
7/5/96	Copy of "What PC"			2-95				
8/5/96	5 reams A4 bond				13-99			
15/5/96	Fares to Uxbridge library					1-60		
20/5/96	Sub to "Library Campaign"							12-00
23/5/96	Pay for FMN info	36-00						
24/5/96	Pay for "Dents Plus"	40-00						

Fig 8. An example of an analysis sheet prepared for taxation purposes.

assessed under Clause II of Schedule D of the Income and Corporation Taxes Act 1988. In this case, if your expenses exceed income, the loss can either be carried forward and set against future income from your freelance writing or set against other income subject to tax in the same year.

Whichever case applies, you will need to submit details of all your writing income to the Inland Revenue. It is therefore important that you keep records of all expenditure related to your writing in order to offset it against your earnings. Whenever you pay for something in connection with your writing business obtain and keep a receipt as proof of such expenditure. Also, make a note in your accounts book. Ensure you make a note of everything. Here is a checklist of deductible items.

- Any expenses in employing secretarial, typing or research services.
- Telephone charges, postage, stationery, pens, pencils, paper, typewriter ribbons, film, photographic processing expenses, maintenance and insurance of your typewriter, photocopier and other office equipment.
- Magazines and books used for market and subject research.
- Travel expenses, hotels, fares, car running expenses including repairs, petrol, oil, garaging, cleaning, parking, road tax, depreciation, insurance, AA/RAC membership.
- Capital allowances for your typewriter, desk, photocopier, filing cabinet.
- The proportion of heating and lighting bills associated with the room used to undertake your writing activities.
- Subscriptions to professional societies and associations.
- Accountancy charges.
- Premiums to a pension scheme.

If you are undertaking your writing as a spare-time activity, alongside other Pay As You Earn employment, you should ensure that associated accounts are kept completely separate from your full-time employment. It is essential not to confuse the two. The Inland Revenue will treat these accounts separate from any other employment.

Under certain circumstances a writer may spread lump sum receipts over two or three tax years, whenever received, and royalties during two years from the date of first publication or performance of work. Those in the fortunate position of needing to worry about spreading income to reduce their tax liability will often employ an accountant to arrange their financial affairs.

Value Added Tax

When your income is above a certain amount (this level is adjusted from time to time, so check with your local tax office) you will have to register for Value Added Tax (VAT). A business is required to register:

- at the end of any month if the value of taxable supplies in the past 12 months has exceeded the annual threshold
  or
- if there are reasonable grounds for believing that the value of taxable supplies in the next 12 months will exceed the annual threshold.

Once you have registered for VAT you can add the current rate of tax to the price you charge for your writing. You should also keep a record of VAT that you have paid on all expenses incurred during your work as a writer. This can be claimed against your income tax.

Every three months you will need to declare how much VAT you have spent and how much you have been paid. If you have spent more than you have earned you will be reimbursed with the difference. If you have earned more than you have spent you must pay the difference.

Most newcomers to freelance writing who read this book will

be unlikely to have to worry too much about VAT. They simply won't earn enough. If you are fortunate enough to have to register for VAT then I'm sure your income won't feel too much of a dent if you employ the services of an accountant.

Index